Fabulously Gluten Free

A Collection of Gluten Free Recipes

By: Gail Friesen

Tasted by: Terry Friesen

Order this book online at www.trafford.com
or email orders@trafford.com

Most Trafford titles are also available at major online book retailers.

Printed in Victoria, BC, Canada.

ISBN: 978-1-4269-1852-0 (sc)
ISBN: 978-1-4269-1853-7 (hc)

Library of Congress Control Number: 2009938457

*Our mission is to efficiently provide the world's finest, most comprehensive book publishing
service, enabling every author to experience success. To find out how to publish your book, your
way, and have it available worldwide, visit us online at www.trafford.com*

Trafford rev. 1/29/10

 www.trafford.com

North America & international
toll-free: 1 888 232 4444 (USA & Canada)
phone: 250 383 6864 ✦ fax: 812 355 4082

Table of Contents

Dedication

This recipe book is dedicated to my husband Terry, for his patience and willingness to taste/eat whatever I built, and to my parents for the passing on to me the persistence gene...........

And to my sister Joanne McDonald and my friends, Marie Hemstock and Pam Egert for their support in bringing this book together.

Also, $2 from every book sold will be donated to The Canadian Celiac Association to support   persons with celiac disease.

Introduction

In our house, I am not a celiac; my husband is. Early on in our relationship we decided that it would be much easier for him if we tried to keep things in our house to a gluten free standard. This does not mean that I do not periodically bring in a few items, but it does mean that I have had to adjust, especially in the preparing of meals, as the outcome did not always turn out/taste to what I am accustomed to. So... I set out to develop a cookbook that anyone can use, the outcome/taste is a delicious one, easy access to the ingredients and to manage time spent cooking. My husband naturally took on the role as official taster...

On the following pages is the outcome of our efforts; I hope you enjoy these recipes as much as we do. You will notice that I have a space on the bottom of each recipe for your own comments, what works well for you or changes you would like to try the next time.

Gail

Hints and Watch-outs

- **Read the label; read the label; read the label:**

  Manufacturers do not necessarily put in the same ingredients time after time. They may change – please don't be complacent, read the label every time you purchase a product. A little gluten is too much.

- **GF indicates Gluten Free product or item:**

  GF in front of items indicates where there is possibility of non-compliance with a gluten free diet. The safest way to ensure compliance to a gluten free diet is to read the label on all items you are cooking with and/or purchasing at the market.

- **Food preparation:**
  - Avoid contamination with products which contain gluten.
  - Always use a clean surface, utensil, pan or pot.
  - When preparing something that is gluten free ensure there is no cross contamination between gluten free products and those containing gluten (including oil used to cook foods).
  - Ensure items that may be shared between users – ensure there is no cross contamination between products where implements could transfer bread crumbs, e.g. jam, honey, mayonnaise, butter, margarine containers, etc. This also includes sharing measuring cups, flour sifters, etc.
  - To avoid cross contamination is to ensure that the gluten free meal items are prepared before items containing gluten.
  - Keep handy a container of All Purpose Gluten Free Flour Mixture, (see the GF Flour section of this book for the recipe) this will save time in pulling out various flours. Also, this has proven to be a foundation in my modifying of recipes.

- **Where to find GF products:**

  As the awareness of Celiac disease has increased there may be stores specializing in your area, so looking through your local yellow pages or surfing the internet may help you find these stores, some other places to find gluten free products are:
  - Specialty areas of the grocery store,
  - The ethnic section of your grocery store (e.g. Asian, East Indian sections) or communities and their markets,
  - Health food stores,
  - Shopping on the Internet,
  - There is a lot of information available on the Celiac diet. A good source for information is your local chapter of the Canadian Celiac Association.

- Cookie dough can be made and frozen for future occasions; roll cookie dough into long rolls and cover well with cellophane, and wrap in a self sealing bag and when the cookie craving hits, your cooking time is cut in half. I recommend freezing for no more than two months.

- Pie dough can also be made and frozen for future occasions; flatten into 4 x 4 squares, wrap well (plastic wrap and then a freezer bag) and freeze. Recommend freezing for no more than two months. When thawing out, leave dough in plastic wrap to prevent drying out of the dough.

- If you have a bread maker, a time saving tip is to make ahead bags of the required GF flour for GF bread. This speeds up the process vs. having to pull out each individual type of flour. I suggest keeping these pre-made packages in the refrigerator, take them out two hours prior to use so they are at room temperature and give the bag of flour a stir prior to adding it to the bread machine.

- If you don't have a meat thermometer, you should have one. For safety reasons, and to ensure meat is cooked to the desired state, you simply should have one.

- Use a candy thermometer; it takes the guesswork out of making sauces for things like GF puffed rice squares.

- Parchment paper is a valuable commodity in our house. I use it for covering my cookie sheets to prevent sticking and makes clean up a breeze. Discard the parchment paper and quick wipe the cookie sheets with a damp cloth.

- When working with dough made of gluten free flour there is a tendency for it to be sticky and it may not come off the working surface easily; one trick is to use a large sheet of parchment paper and roll the product on the parchment paper. This saves time and frustration with the product being made (e.g. piecrust, rollout onto the parchment paper and then flip it into the pie dish).

- Toothpick test: is when a toothpick is inserted in a couple of spots over the cake being cooked and comes out clean. If cake pieces stick to the toothpick, some additional cooking time may be required.

- Save all ends, pieces of gluten free bread, or waffles. I break up the bread, waffles in to smaller pieces and save these in an airtight container in the freezer. These can be used in making hamburgers, saved for making a stuffing, toppings on casseroles, etc.

- Eggs, for all of these recipes, I use large eggs. I like the added moisture.

- Ensure that all gluten free products are stored in separate containers to ensure you prevent cross contamination with other non-gluten free products in your home.

- Be cautious when buying gluten free products from the bulk food bins. It is difficult to ensure that scoops used have not been used in other non-gluten free bins, which may result in cross contamination.

Gluten Containing Ingredients

This is **not** a comprehensive list as some items may have changed or been added to the list from the time I pulled this information together. Please check with the Canadian Celiac Association or your local Celiac Society for most up-to-date information

Grain Sources

Barley

Bulgur

Couscous

Graham flour

Modified wheat starch

Rye

Wheat

Wheat bran

Wheat germ

Wheat starch

Derived from Barley

Dinkel

Durum

Einkorn

Emmer

Faro

Kamut

Malt (is a cereal grain usually barley, which has been soaked, germinated and dried)

Malt extract

Malt flavouring

Malt syrup

Malt vinegar

Semolina

Spelt

Hidden Sources of Gluten

Hydrolyzed vegetable protein (HVP)

Hydrolyzed plant protein (HPP)

Food starch (the source of food starch is unknown)

GF non-stick spray (may contain wheat or alcohol – read the label)

Substitutions Ideas

If you can't find some of these items gluten free, or you can't find the item here are some alternatives:

Recipe Calls for:	Consideration Using:
Dry mustard	Dijon mustard or prepared mustard (1 tsp to 1 tbsp)
Xanthan gum	Guar gum
Sake	Cooking sherry
Rolled oats	Slivered almonds or Rolled rice
Puffed wheat	Puffed rice
Malt vinegar	Red wine vinegar
Worcestershire sauce	Mix together: 1 tsp brown sugar, splash of lime juice, 1 tsp GF soya sauce, 1 tsp cider or white vinegar, dash hot pepper sauce, pinch cloves
Capers	Chopped spicy dill pickles (1 tbsp to 1 tbsp)
Wasbi	Hot Horseradish (I use 1 tsp or horseradish to 1 tsp wasbi)
Chilli paste	Hot red pepper flakes (1 tbsp to ¼ tsp or to your taste)
Buttermilk	Milk with lemon juice (1 cup is equal to 1 cup of milk and 1 tbsp of lemon juice)
Hoisin sauce	GF soya sauce

Cooking for High Altitudes

Adjustments in Baking:

Two adjustments are needed:

1. Increase cooking time for boiled or simmered foods

2. Change proportions in the ingredients used for dishes that rise during baking, such as cakes and bread. At times, it is necessary to adjust baking temperatures.

At high altitude, water boils at a lower temperature than at sea level. It therefore takes longer to reach the internal temperature needed to cook food.

Oven temperatures are not affected by altitude changes. However, since the atmospheric pressure decreases at high altitude, dough rises more rapidly during baking than at sea level. The rising period for yeast breads will also be shorter.

Adjustments of oven temperature at high altitude:

Increase by 25 F (15 C) 3,500 feet and above (1000 meters)

Measures

Conventional Measurements	Metric (Standard Measure)
Spoons:	Millilitres
1/8 teaspoon (tsp)	0.5 ml
¼ tsp	1.0 ml
½ tsp	2 ml
1 tsp	5 ml
2 tsp	10 ml
1 tablespoon (tbsp)	15 ml
Wet Measures:	
Cup (C) Millilitres	
¼ cup (C)	60 ml
1/3 C	75 ml
½ C	125 ml
2/3 C	150 ml
¾ C	175 ml
1 C	250 ml

Dry Measures:

Ounces (oz.)	Grams (g)
1 oz.	28 g
2 oz	57 g
3 oz	85 g
5 oz	125 g
6 oz	140 g
7 oz	200g
8 oz	250 g
16 oz	500 g
32 oz	1000 g

Conventional Measurements	**Metric (Standard Measure)**
Pan Sizes: Conventional - Inches	Metric – Centimetres
Square Pans	
8 x 8	20 x 20
9 x 9	22 x 22
Rectangular Pans	
7 x 11 x 1 ½	28 x 17 x 3.7
9 x 13 x 1 ¾	34 x 23 x 4
10 x 15 x ¾	40 x 25 x 2
12 x 8 x 1 ¾	30 x 19 x 4.5
14 x 17 x ¾	43 x 45 x 2

Appetizers

Bacon Wrapped Dates Stuffed with Almonds:

Whole blanched almonds, toasted	24
Dates, medium and pitted	24
Bacon, thin slices	8

(Cut each slice into three)

- Preheat oven to 350°F (180°C)
- Stuff an almond inside each date
- Wrap a slice of bacon around the date and almond
- Secure it with a toothpick
- Bake for 20 – 30 minutes or until the bacon is crisp
- Serve warm
- Serves 8 (3 per person) or yields 24

Notes:

➤ To toast the almonds, spread on a baking sheet and bake at 350°F (180°C) for approximately 4 - 5 minutes, they should be a light brown in color.

➤ The bacon wrapped dates can be frozen for approximately one month; to freeze do not cook the bacon wrapped dates, lay them out on a cookie sheet and place in freezer for one hour, remove and place in an air tight container. To use, thaw and follow the above cooking directions.

Baked Garlic:

Garlic, large heads	3	
Olive oil	¼ C	60 ml

- Preheat oven to 325°F (160°C)
- Remove any of the loose paper-like skin from the garlic head
- Slice the top of the garlic head off and drizzle with olive oil
- Wrap in foil and poke a few holes in the foil to permit the steam to escape, (or use garlic baker if you have one)
- Bake for 1 1/4 hours, until garlic is soft
- Remove from oven and serve with crackers
- Serves: 6 – 8

Notes:
➢ Rule of thumb is one head of garlic for 2 people.
➢ Other serving options: spread on crackers cream cheese and top with a baked garlic clove; if using brie cheese, heat brie in the oven until it begins to slightly melt, cover cracker with brie and baked garlic clove.

Black Bean Dip:

GF non-stick spray

Onion, chopped	½ C	125 ml
Garlic, minced	2 cloves	
Salsa	½ C	125 ml
Chilli powder	½ tsp	2 ml
Ground cumin	½ tsp	2 ml
Black beans	19 oz. can	540 ml
Cilantro	¼ tsp	1 ml
Monterey Jack cheese, shredded	¼ C	60 ml
Lime juice	1 tbsp	15 ml

- Pour the black beans and liquid into a bowl and break them into smaller pieces with a fork, this makes it easier for dipping

- Spray a large non-stick skillet with GF non-stick spray and warm skillet over medium heat

- Add onion and sauté until tender

- Add in garlic and sauté for 2- 3 minutes; be careful not to burn the garlic

- Reduce the heat to medium low. Add to the non-stick skillet mashed black beans, salsa, Chilli powder, and ground cumin; cook for approximately 5 minutes or until thick, stirring constantly

- Remove from heat and add cheese, cilantro, and lime juice, stirring until cheese melts Serve warm or at room temperature

- Serve with GF tortilla chips

- Yield: 1 2/3 cups (serving size: 2 tablespoons).

Bruschetta:

Ingredient	Amount	Metric
Tomatoes, large chopped	3	
Dried basil	1 tsp	5 ml
Parmesan cheese	5 tbsp	75 ml
Olive Oil	4 tbsp	60 ml
Garlic, crushed	4 cloves	
Oregano	1 tsp	5 ml
Seasoning salt	to taste	
Ground black pepper	to taste	
GF bread	1 loaf	

- In a medium sized bowl combine tomatoes, dried basil, Parmesan cheese, olive oil, garlic, oregano, seasoning salt and ground black pepper. Cover and let stand for one hour before serving. The flavour intensifies as the mixture sits; I like to make a few hours prior to serving

- Preheat oven when using the broiler feature

- Slice the loaf of gluten free bread into sections and brush each piece with a bit of olive oil

- Toast under the broiler until light brown

- Remove from broiler and then spread over each section some of the tomato mixture

- Yield: 3 cups

Notes:
- Another option is to serve this as a dip and serve with nacho chips
- Small pizza shells heated and sliced into sections (e.g. 8) also make a great serving alternative to a loaf of GF bread

Cheese Ball:

Cream cheese, softened	8 oz	250 ml
Sour cream	¼ C	60 ml
Cheddar cheese, sharp, shredded	3 C	750 ml
(Reserve 1 C for presentation)		
Onion, chopped	3 tbsp	45 ml
Cayenne pepper	½ tsp	2 ml
Paprika	dash	
Hot sauce (e.g. Tabasco)	dash	
Dill weed	dash	
Garlic powder	dash	

- In a medium sized mixing bowl, beat cream cheese until smooth.
- 2 C (500 ml) of cheddar cheese, chopped onion, cayenne pepper; paprika, hot sauce (e.g. Tabasco), dill weed and garlic power and blend together
- Wrap in plastic wrap and place in refrigerator until cool
- Remove from wrap, form into a ball and roll in remaining cheddar cheese, and serve with gluten free crackers

Cheese Puffs:

Water	1 C	250 ml
Margarine or butter	1/3 C	75 ml
GF flour mixture	1 C	250 ml
Eggs, large	4	
Cheddar cheese	1 ½ C	375 ml
(Sharp or medium)		
Dijon mustard	1 tsp	5 ml

- Preheat oven to 400°F (200 °C)

- Grease cookie sheet

- Combine water and butter in a heavy saucepan and bring to a boil

- Remove from heat and add the GF flour mixture all at once

- Beat with a wooden spoon until well mixed

- Return to medium heat and beat until mixture leaves sides of pan and forms a ball

- Remove from heat and beat in eggs one at a time to form a smooth mixture (this takes some time so be patient), beat thoroughly

- Stir in cheese, and mustard (see variations list below for additional ideas)

- Drop by small teaspoonfuls onto a greased cookie sheet

- Bake for 15 –20 minutes

- Makes approximately 24 puffs

➤ These can be frozen for a month or two. To serve: reheat in oven (350°F/180 °C) for approximately 5 – 10 minutes – until warm.

Variations:

Green onions chopped (4 green onions chopped)

Ham chopped (1 cup/250 ml)

Crispy bacon (1 cup/250 ml)

Cheese Crispies:

Margarine or butter	1 C	250 ml
GF flour mixture	2 C	500 ml
Cheddar cheese, sharp, shredded	2 C	500 ml
Xanthan gum	2 tsp	10 ml
Cayenne pepper	½ tsp	2 ml
Tabasco sauce	3 drops	
Parmesan cheese, grated	½ C	125 ml
GF rice crispies (cereal)	1 C	250 ml

- Preheat oven to 325°F (160°C)
- In a large mixing bowl combine all ingredients; stir (may require some mixing by hand) until well blended
- Wrap this mixture in plastic wrap for 30 minutes
- After the mixture is chilled, form dough in to 1-inch (2.5-cm) balls and place on a lightly greased baking sheet
- Using a fork dipped in GF flour mixture, flatten each ball in a criss-cross pattern
- Bake for 12 – 15 minutes or until lightly browned
- Remove from pan and cool on a wire rack
- Serve immediately or store in an airtight container
- Yield: 3 dozen cheese crispies

Crab Dip:

Ingredient	Imperial	Metric
Light cream cheese	8 oz	250 g
Light mayonnaise	½ C	125 ml
Light sour cream	½ C	125 ml
Parmesan cheese, divided	½ C	125 ml
Monterey Jack or mozzarella cheese	½ C	125 ml
Crab meat	1 can	170 g
Garlic, minced	2 cloves	
Black pepper	¼ tsp	1 ml
Onion powder	½ tsp	2 ml

- Preheat oven to 350°F (180°C)
- In a large bowl, combine light cream cheese, mayonnaise, and sour cream, blend well
- Add parmesan cheese, reserving 2 tbsp (30 ml), Monterey Jack cheese, crab meat, garlic, black pepper and onion powder, stirring until well blended
- Spoon mixture into a 1 quart (1 litre) baking dish
- Sprinkle with 2 tbsp (30 ml) of Parmesan cheese
- Bake for 30 minutes or until bubbly and golden brown
- Yield: 3 ½ C (875 ml)

Green Onion Cakes:

GF flour mixture	3 1/3 C	750 ml
Water, boiling	1 ¼ C	310 ml
Xanthan gum	1 tbsp	15 ml
Sesame oil	2 tsp	10 ml
Green onions, chopped	1 C	250 ml
Salt	2 tsp	10 ml
Pepper	½ tsp	2 ml
Cooking oil		

Dipping Sauce:

Chicken broth	½ C	125 ml
GF soya sauce	2 tbsp	30 ml
Green onion, minced	2 tsp	10 ml
Garlic, minced	1 tsp	5 ml
Chilli sauce	1 tsp	5 ml
Cooking oil	¼ C	60 ml

- In a large bowl, place GF flour mixture, xanthan gum, and boiling water, stirring with a fork until dough is evenly moistened
- On a lightly floured board using GF flour, knead dough until smooth and satiny, about 5 minutes
- Cover and let rest for 30 minutes
- Combine ingredients for dipping sauce in a bowl

- Lightly flour working surface with GF flour, roll dough into a cylinder, cut into 12 equal portions

- Brush each portion of dough with a thin film of cooking oil. Sprinkle with a small portion of sesame oil, green onions, salt and pepper

- Roll a portion of dough into an 8 inch circle about 1/8 inch thick; keep the remaining dough covered to prevent drying

- Heat up a wide frying pan over medium heat

- Add 2 tbsp (30 ml) of cooking oil; be sure to cover the whole pan and sides

- Add 1 cake and cook turning once, until gold brown (2 –3 minutes on each side)

- Remove and drain on paper towels; repeat for each cake

- Cut into wedges and serve with dipping sauce

- Yield: 24 cakes

Ham and Cream Cheese Dip:

Can of flakes of ham	6.5 oz	184 g
Light cream cheese	1 C	125 ml
Horseradish sauce	2 tsp	10 ml

- In a medium sized mixing bowl, open a can of flaked ham put into bowl and mash into fine texture

- Add in the cream cheese to the ham and blend together well

- Add in horseradish to the cream cheese and ham mixture and blend again

- Cover and place in refrigerator to sit for two hours prior to use; the flavour intensifies, as the mixture sits, I like to make about 2 hours before serving

- Serve with crackers or as a topping for rolls,

- Yield: 1 cup (250 ml)

Mushroom Caps with Crabmeat:

Can of crabmeat	6.5 oz	113 g
Light cream cheese	8 oz pkg	250 ml
Garlic, minced	1 clove	
Mozzarella cheese, shredded	1 C	250 ml
Mushrooms, large	24	

- Preheat oven to 350°F (180°C)
- Clean mushrooms and remove stem and place on plate and cover with a dry paper towel to absorb any extra moisture from the cleaning
- In a medium sized bowl mix the cream cheese, crab and garlic together
- Stuff the mushroom caps with the crab mixture and then sprinkle with the mozzarella cheese; place the completed stuffed mushrooms in a large oven proof baking dish
- Bake covered for 10 minutes, remove cover and cook for an additional 10 minutes or until golden brown
- Remove from the oven and serve
- Serves: 8

Shrimp with Chilli Lime:

Shrimp, pre-cooked, thawed and peeled,	1 1g	454 g
Garlic, minced	2 cloves	
Butter	2 tbsp	30 ml
Lime juice or juice from a lime	¼ C	60 ml
Tabasco or Chilli sauce	¼ tsp	1 ml

- Thaw and peel pre-cooked shrimp

- Mince garlic

- In a large frying pan, over medium heat melt the butter, then add the minced garlic.

- Add to the butter mixture the lime juice, and Tabasco or Chilli sauce, stir together and then add in the pre-cooked, peeled shrimp.

- Cook this mixture approximately 3 – 5 minutes until hot

- Place on a small platter, and serve warm

Spinach and Artichoke Dip:

Mozzarella, shredded part-skim	2 C	500 ml
Sour cream	½ C	125 ml
Parmesan cheese	¼ C	60 ml
Black pepper	¼ tsp	1 ml
Garlic, crushed	3 cloves	
Artichoke hearts, drained and chopped	12 oz	340 ml
Light cream cheese, softened	8 oz pkg	250 ml
Spinach, thawed, drained, squeezed dry, and chopped	5 oz	162 g
GF Tortilla chips for dipping		

- Preheat oven to 350°F (180°C)

- Combine 1 ½ C (375 ml) mozzarella cheese, sour cream, 2 tbsp (30 ml) Parmesan cheese, and black pepper, crushed garlic, chopped and drained artichoke hearts, light cream cheese, drained and chopped spinach; stir until well blended

- Spoon mixture into a 1 quart (1 litre) baking dish

- Sprinkle with ½ C (125 ml) mozzarella cheese and 2 tbsp of Parmesan cheese

- Bake for 30 minutes or until bubbly and golden brown

- Serve hot and with the GF Tortilla chips for dipping

- Yield: 5 ½ C (1375 ml)

Breads, Pancakes, Waffles

Blue Corn Tortillas

— get "Tortillas" $5 Cookbook Dr. Tena Friesen

2c blue corn meal
1/4 tsp salt
1 c warm water

1. Mix (until cornmeal well moistened).
2. Cover w/ plastic wrap.
3. Roll ≈ 1/4 c. of mixture into a ball &
   roll flat w/ a rolling pin on lightly floured surface.
4. Let tortilla stand for 1 or 2 min.
5. Fry in lightly oiled pan over med heat ≈ 30 sec/side
6. Serve hot (as chips or for hard tacos)

Sushi Style Roll Ups (Pg 12) — serves 3

2c warm cooked rice
2 Tbsp rice vinegar
3oz cream cheese

1 tsp whipped horseradish
3 flour tortillas (see recipe)
1 cucumber — → 1/4 lengthwise
remove seeds, slice each 1/2 into 3 thin slices
Roasted red pepper

1. Mix rice + vinegar, cover & refridge. 30 min
2. mix cream cheese & horseradish
3. Place tortilla on plastic wrap.
4. 2 Tbsps cream cheese mixture spread on tortilla. each
5. 1/3 c. rice mixture across centre.
6. 1 strip cuc down centre + roasted pepper strips.
7. 1/3 c rice mixture on top.
8. roll. Refridge 4 hrs. Slice into 8 3/4" thick slices

All Purpose Gluten Free Flour Mixture:

This flour concoction has proven to be a valuable asset in our house. Whenever a recipe calls for flour, this flour is used.

GF potato flour or starch	3 C	750 ml
GF soya flour	2 C	500 ml
GF rice flour	2 C	500 ml
GF Cornstarch	1 C	250 ml

- Mix together potato flour, soya flour, rice flour and cornstarch

- Store mixture in the refrigerator in a sealed container, e.g. ice cream container. This mixture can be stored for up to 3 months

- As this flour mixture settles, ensure it is stirred well prior to each use

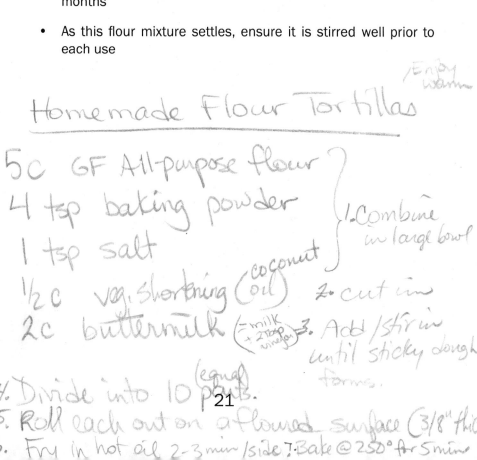

Enjoy warm

Homemade Flour Tortillas

5 c GF All-purpose flour
4 tsp baking powder
1 tsp salt
½ c veg. shortening (coconut oil)
2 c buttermilk (= milk + 2 tbsp vinegar)

1. Combine in large bowl
2. cut in
3. Add/stir in until sticky dough forms.
4. Divide into 10 equal parts.
5. Roll each out on a floured surface (3/8" thick)
6. Fry in hot oil 2-3 min /side 7. Bake @ 250° for 5 min

Baked French Toast:

This recipe is made the night before it is required.

GF bread	12 slices	
Eggs, large	5	
Milk	2 ½ C	625 ml
Brown sugar, packed	1 C	250 ml
(Reserve ¼ C for topping)		
Vanilla	1 tsp	5 ml
Cinnamon	1 tsp	5 ml
Pecans, roughly chopped	1 C	250 ml
Butter or margarine, melted	¼ C	60 ml
Blueberries, fresh or frozen	2 C	500 ml

- Grease a 13 x 9 x 1 ¾ inches (34 x 23 x 4 cm) baking dish, layout the bread in the dish.
- In a medium bowl combine eggs, milk, ¾ C of brown sugar, vanilla and cinnamon, and pour over the bread
- Cover and refrigerate for 8 hours or overnight
- Remove from refrigerator 30 minutes before baking
- Preheat oven to 400°F (200°C)
- Top with chopped pecans
- Combine butter and remaining ¼ C of brown sugar and pour over top of the bread
- Bake uncovered for 25 minutes

- Remove from the oven and top with blueberries. Bake for an additional 10 minutes or until a toothpick is inserted into the middle of the mixture and it comes out clean

- Remove from oven and serve

- Serves: 6 – 8

Blueberry Pancakes:

Eggs, large	2	
Butter/Margarine, melted	2 tbsp	30 ml
Milk	1 ¼ C	310 ml
GF all purpose flour mixture	2 C	500 ml
Xanthan gum	2 tsp	10 ml
Granulated sugar	1 tbsp	15 ml
GF baking powder	1 tbsp	15 ml
Salt	½ tsp	2 ml
Blueberries (fresh or frozen)	½ C	125 ml
GF non-stick spray		

- Spray griddle or frying pan with GF non-stick spray, and preheat
- In a large bowl beat eggs lightly, then mix in milk, melted butter or margarine, and stir together
- Mix in the GF all-purpose flour mixture, xanthan gum, granulated sugar, GF baking powder, and salt
- Add blueberries and stir
- Pour onto griddle or frying pan, using approximately 2 tbsp (30 ml) of pancake mix per pancake
- Cook until bubbles form on topside of pancake and then flip over (flipping only once) cook until a light golden brown
- Yield: approximately 24 pancakes

Cheese Soufflé:

Butter	3 tbsp	45 ml
Milk – skim or 2% (hot milk)	2 C	500 ml
Eggs, large (separated)	4	
GF flour mixture	1/3 C	75 ml
Cheese, grated	1/3 C	75 ml
Tabasco Sauce	dash	
Pepper	to taste	
Salt	dash	

GF non stick spray

- Preheat oven to 350°F (180 °C)
- Grease 9 x 9 inch (22 cm) baking dish with GF non stick spray
- In a medium sized bowl, blend together butter and GF flour mixture
- In a small sauce pan heat the milk; be cautious not to scald the milk
- Blend into the butter/GF flour mixture the hot milk, salt, pepper, Tabasco sauce and grated cheese
- Cool slowly
- stirring constantly until cheese is melted and sauce is thick
- In a separate bow beat egg yolks
- In another bowl beat the egg whites until stiff
- Add well-beaten egg yolks and fold in stiffly beaten egg whites
- Pour into a greased baking dish

- Bake for 50 – 60 minutes or until firm to the touch

- Serve at once

- Serves: 8

Note:

➢ You can heat the milk in the microwave, be sure not to scald the milk.

Dumplings:

Granulated sugar	2 tbsp	30 ml
Shortening	3 tbsp	45 ml
Egg, large, beaten	1	
Buttermilk or sour milk	½ C	125 ml
GF all purpose flour mixture	1 C	250 ml
Xanthan gum	1 tsp	5 ml
GF baking powder	2 tsp	10 ml
Baking soda	½ tsp	2 ml
Salt	½ tsp	2 ml

- In a large mixing bowl, blend together sugar and shortening, beaten egg

- In a separate bowl mix together GF flour mixture, xanthan gum, GF baking powder, baking soda and salt

- To the sugar, shortening, egg mixture, add the buttermilk or sour milk while alternating with scoops of the above GF flour mixture; be careful not to over stir, as mixture may become stiff and hard

- Drop the dumpling mixture by small spoonfuls onto the boiling stew

- Cover and return to a simmer for 20 minutes

- Do not peak into pot when they are cooking, as this will cause them not to rise fully

- Serve hot

Note:

➢ To sour the milk, add 1 tsp of lemon juice or vinegar to the milk.

Feathery Pancakes:

GF flour mixture	1 C	250 ml
Granulated sugar	2 tbsp	30 ml
GF baking powder	2 tbsp	30 ml
Salt	½ tsp	2 ml
Xanthan gum	1 tsp	5 ml
Egg, large, beaten	3	
Milk	1 C	250 ml

GF non-stick spray

- Preheat cooking surface (griddle, electric frying pan, etc.)
- Stir GF flour mixture in storage container prior to measuring
- Sift together in a large bowl the GF flour mixture, salt, sugar, GF baking powder and xanthan gum
- Mix in the beaten egg and milk; beat until well blended
- Spray cooking surface with GF non stick spray
- Spoon onto cooking surface approximately 2 tbsp (30 ml) of pancake mixture; cook until bubble for and begin to pop, then flip; watch for a golden brown color
- Serves: 6 – 8, 4-inch pancakes

√ recipe makes LOTS!
(Doubled = 32 pancakes)

28

GF Bread Recipe for a Bread Making Machine:

Water – warm	1 ¼ C	300 ml
Milk – skim or 2%	1 C	250 ml
Eggs, large	3	
Honey (melted)	*¼ c.*	*60 ml*
Canola oil or melted margarine	2 tbsp	30 ml
Vinegar	1 tsp	5 ml
Rice flour	1 ½ C	375 ml
Whole bean flour	2/3 C	150 ml
Tapioca flour	1/3 C	75 ml
Potato starch flour	1/3 C	75 ml
~~Granulated sugar~~ *Gelatin (unflavored)*	~~¼ C~~ *1 tsp*	~~60 ml~~ *5 ml*
Xanthan gum	1 tbsp	15 ml
Nutritional Yeast	*1 Tbsp*	*15 ml*
Salt	2 tsp	10 ml
Yeast, quick rise	1 tbsp	15 ml

- In a bowl whisk together water, milk, eggs, oil and vinegar until well blended and pour into baking pan of the bread maker

- Place the following ingredients in order on top of the liquid ingredients: rice flour, whole bean flour, tapioca flour, potato starch flour, granulated sugar, xanthan gum, salt and yeast

- Insert the baking pan into the baking unit

- On the bread maker select the bread type button, regular loaf and then push start

- During the first 5 minutes of the mixing sequence the sides of the pan should be scraped down to assist with the mixing; close lid

Choose #2 Program = Quick Bread (1:28hrs)

29

(Leave in maker ≈ +10 min after cooking to firm up + cool down)

- Once the machine indicates it is done, remove the baking pan using oven mitts *(leave in bread maker a 10 more mins to cool down t finish cook)*

- Remove bread from baking pan and set on cooling rack

Notes:

➢ Use exact measurements.

➢ Xanthan gum gives the bread some stretch, an alternate to xanthan gum is guar gum it is the synthetic version of xanthan gum.

➢ Have all the ingredients, with the exception of the water, at room temperature. Ensure the water is warm, not too hot; if too hot will prevent yeast development.

➢ After the initial start of the bread maker (first 5 minutes), scrape down the sides of the container with a rubber spatula to ensure good mixture of the flour.

➢ Expect the ends of the bread to be flat, and the top to be somewhat concave as there is no gluten to hold up the top of the bread.

➢ If the bread ends up with a dip in the center after cooking, next time try removing two tablespoons of water, and increase the salt by ½ a teaspoon.

GF Cinnamon Raisin Bread - Bread Making Machine:

Water – warm	1 ¼ C	300 ml
Milk – skim or 2%	1 C	250 ml
Honey	¼ C	60ml
Eggs, large	3	
Canola oil or melted margarine	2 tbsp	30 ml
Vinegar	1 tsp	5 ml
Rice flour	1 ½ C	375 ml
Whole bean flour	2/3 C	150 ml
Tapioca flour	1/3 C	75 ml
Potato starch flour	1/3 C	75 ml
unflavored gelatin	1 tsp	5ml (optional)
Sultana raisins	1/3 C	75 ml
nutritional yeast	1 Tbsp	(optional)
Granulated sugar	¼ C	60 ml (add as honey w/ liquid ingredients)
Xanthan gum	1 tbsp	15 ml
Salt	2 tsp	10 ml
Cinnamon	1 ½ tsp	7 ml
Yeast, quick rise,	1 pkg	

- In a bowl whisk together water, milk, eggs, oil and vinegar until well blended; pour into baking pan of the bread maker

- Place the following ingredients in order on top of the liquid ingredients: rice flour, whole bean flour, tapioca flour, potato starch flour, sultana raisins, granulated sugar, xanthan gum, salt, cinnamon and yeast

- Insert the baking pan into the baking unit

- On the bread maker select the bread type button, regular loaf and then push start (#2 Program = 1:28 hrs)

31

- During the first 5 minutes of the mixing sequence the sides of the pan should be scraped with a rubber spatula down to assist with the mixing; close lid

- Once the machine indicates it is done, remove the baking pan using oven mitts

- Remove bread from baking pan and set on cooling rack

Notes:

➢ Use exact measurements.

➢ Xanthan gum gives the bread some stretch, an alternate to xanthan gum is guar gum it is the synthetic version of xanthan gum.

➢ Have all the ingredients, with the exception of the water, at room temperature. Ensure the water is warm, not too hot; if too hot will prevent yeast development.

➢ After the initial start of the bread maker (first 5 minutes), scrape down the sides of the container with a rubber spatula to ensure good mixture of the flour.

➢ Expect the ends of the bread to be flat, and the top to be somewhat concave as there is no gluten to hold up the top of the bread.

➢ If the bread ends up with a dip in the center after cooking, next time try removing two tablespoons of water, and increase the salt by ½ a teaspoon.

Marg's Belgium Waffles:

Eggs, large	6	
Sour cream, light	1 C	250 ml
Butter/Margarine, melted	1/3 C	75 ml
Milk	1 1/2 C	375 ml
Vanilla	1 tsp	5 ml
Corn flour	2 C	500 ml
Granulated sugar	2 tbsp	30 ml
GF baking powder	1 tbsp	15 ml
Xanthan gum	1 tbsp	15 ml
GF non-stick spray		

- Preheat waffle iron

- In a large bowl beat eggs lightly

- Mix in sour cream, melted butter or margarine, milk and vanilla, stir together

- Add in corn flour, Granulated sugar, baking powder, and xanthan gum and mix together well. Mixture should have a pancake type consistency

- Spray waffle maker surface with GF non stick spray

- Pour onto the hot waffle iron and remove when waffle is golden brown

- Yield: makes approximately 6 waffles.

Mom's GF Bread Stuffing: See pg 196 GFG

A traditional bread dressings, serve with chicken or turkey (10 – 12 lbs or 4.53 – 5.44 kg's)

Margarine or Butter	¼ C	60 ml
GF Breadcrumbs (or bread crumbled)	12 C	1500 ml
Onion, large, chopped	1	
Brown sugar, packed	¼ C	65 ml
Savory	1 tsp	5 ml
Sage	1 tsp	5 ml
Salt	1/2 tsp	2 ml
Pepper	1/4 tsp	1 ml

- Preheat oven to 350°F (180°C)

- In a large bowl pour in 12 C or 1500 ml of GF bread crumbs

- On medium heat, melt margarine or butter and sauté onions, until transparent

- Mix in the onion mixture, the brown sugar and stir in to ensure distribution

- Add in spices - savory, sage, salt and pepper to onion mixture

- Remove onion mixture from stove and pour over breadcrumbs

- Mix thoroughly

- Check mixture for flavour, if adding more spices be cautious as flavours do intensify when cooked. Mixture may require additional moisture, add water in small amounts to obtain right consistency if not sticking together.

- Put in ovenproof dish and cover with foil or lid, bake for 1 hour at 350°F (180°C)

- Serves: 6 – 8

<u>Notes:</u>

➢ Save all ends from loafs of GF bread, waffles, or other bread products and freeze, use when required to make stuffing. The mixture of the texture and flavours with the variety of bread pieces adds additional flavour.

Mother-In-Law's Popovers (Yorkshire Puddings):

GF all purpose flour mixture	1 C	250 ml
Salt	1/2 tsp	2 ml
Xanthan gum	1 tsp	5 ml
Egg, large	3	
Milk	1 C	250 ml
Oil	1 tbsp	15 ml
GF non-stick spray		

- Pre-heat oven to 450°F (230°C)

- Pre-heat muffin tins prior to filling

- In a blender add: milk, eggs, and oil. Blend at high speed until well blended

- Add the GF flour mixture, salt and xanthan gum and stir by hand until slightly mixed

- Blend again, briefly, at high speed until the mixture is smooth

- Coat the pre-heated muffin tins with the GF non-stick spray and fill each muffin tin ½ full with the flour mixture

- Bake popovers for 15 minutes at 450°F, then reduce to 350°F (180°C), and cook for another 25 minutes longer or until golden brown

- Before removing the popovers from the oven, prick with a toothpick to let the steam escape

- Serve at once

- Serves: 6 – 8

Notes:

- ➤ When planning your meal, coordinate that you put the popovers' into a hot oven, and so that you do not have to open the door again, or they may drop and you want to keep the oven temperature constant.

- ➤ I take the roast out and let it rest in the roasting pan, and then I put in the popovers.

Perogies:

Dough:

GF flour mixture	2 ¾ C	
Salt	1 tsp	5 ml
Xanthan gum	3 tsp	15 ml
Cottage cheese, creamed	1 C	250 ml
Egg, large	1	
Milk	3 tbsp	45 ml
Oil	1 tbsp	15 ml

- In a large bowl put in GF flour, salt, and xanthan gum, mix together
- Make a well in the flour mixture
- Blend together the cottage cheese, egg, milk and oil
- Add this mixture to the well in the flour mixture. Knead well, and then let the dough rest for approximately 1 hour
- Roll out on an oiled cutting board, or other non-stick surface, NOTE the GF flour mixture tends to be sticker than other flours
- Cut round circles with a glass or cookie cutter and then place in the center of the circle of dough a teaspoonful of filling, ensuring mixture does not touch the edges,
- Gently fold the dough/filling mixture in half and pinch sides together, sealing in the filling mixture
- Place completed perogies on a tea towel and cover with a damp second tea towel to prevent drying out.

To cook:

- Bring to boil a pot of salted water and 1 tbsp of cooking oil.

- Add in perogies and gently stir; cook for 4 - 5 minutes. Strain then run cold water over and drain again.

To freeze:

- Place individual perogies on trays in freezer, once frozen, remove from tray and put in an airtight container or plastic bags until required.

- These can be frozen for approximately two months.

Fillings Options:

Cottage Cheese:

Cottage cheese, dry	2 C	500 ml
Egg, large	1	
Salt	pinch	
Pepper	pinch	

- Mix together until it holds shape.

Potato:

Potatoes, cooked and mashed	2 C	500 ml
Vegetable oil	2 tbsp	30 ml
Onions, chopped and fried	2 tbsp	30 ml
Bacon, chopped and fried	2 tbsp	30 ml

- In a medium sized bowl, blend together mashed potatoes, vegetable oil, onion and bacon.
- Mix together until it holds shape. (Test is to squeeze the amount that would go into a Perogie in the palm of your hand to see if it holds shape).

Notes:

➢ Perogies can be served with a variety of toppings or combination of items, for example: sour cream, chopped fried onions, chopped fried bacon, melted butter or margarine. Experiment to see what you like.

➢ When I have gone to friend's homes they have made their perogies with a fruit filling (e.g. strawberry jam) and then serve with whipped cream and/or tossed with some sugar and serve as a dessert.

Pie Crust, Tender Vinegar Pastry:

GF flour mixture	2 ½ C	625 ml
Xanthan gum	1 tbsp	15 ml
Salt	1 tsp	5 ml
Granulated sugar	1 tbsp	15 ml
Shortening (butter, margarine)	¾ C	
Vinegar	2 tbsp	30 ml
Egg, large	1	
Cold water	½ C	60 ml

- Stir GF flour mixture in storage container prior to measuring.

- Sift together in a large bowl the GF flour mixture, salt, sugar, and xanthan gum.

- Cut in the shortening with a knife or pastry blender.

- In another bowl blend together the vinegar, egg and cold water.

- Add this mixture to the flour mixture and blend together. Knead this mixture into a ball, and then divide into two equal portions. If mixture seems to dry, slowly addition additional water in small increments until you have a mixture that holds together

- This dough is a bit more difficult to handle. Chill prior to use, this aids in the handling of this dough and helps the dough remain tender.

- Roll out on parchment paper, or on plastic wrap. Sprinkle with GF flour mixture and then roll out to size of a 9 inch/ 22 cm pie plate. Either of these methods will assist in transferring the dough to the pie plate.

- To bake the crust, cook in a preheated oven of 450°F (230°C). for 10 to 12 minutes.

- To use pie dough later, divide dough recipe in half and shape each section into a 4 x 4 square. Then individually cover in plastic wrap and then store again in another bag, and place in the freezer. This dough can be stored up to 2 months.

- When thawing the dough ensure to leave it wrapped in the plastic wrap to prevent drying.

Tempura Batter:

Ice water	1 C	250 ml
Egg, large	1	
GF flour mixture	1 C	250 ml
Xanthan gum	1 tsp	5 ml
Salt	1 tsp	5 ml

Tempura:

- In a large bowl beat egg, stir in ice water, add flour, salt and xanthan gum and mix lightly

Suggestions for Dipping in the Tempura:

Shrimp,

White fish,

Potatoes,

Sweet potatoes – thinly sliced

Carrots – thinly sliced,

Onions – onion rings

Mushrooms,

Zucchini – thinly sliced

The Dipping Process:

- Heat 2 – 3 inches (7.5 cm) of vegetable oil in a large Dutch oven

- Dip the vegetables or other item into the batter, one at a time, coat well and lower gently into the oil. Don't over crowd the pan

- Fry until golden brown, turn over until done; NEVER leave the Dutch oven unattended while cooking

- Drain on paper towels and serve immediately. As a nice compliment serve with a teriyaki a sauce

- Yield: 6 servings (4 – 5 pieces each)

Meat Dishes

Baked Ham:

Whole ham, bone in	8 – 10 lbs	4 – 5 Kg
Water	2 C	500 ml
Maple Syrup	1 C	250 ml

- Pre-heat oven to 325°F (160°C)

- Put ham in large roasting pan, fat side up

- Mix water and maple syrup and pour over the ham.

- Cover and cook the ham for 1 ½ - 2 hours, depending on size of ham – cook until internal temperature registers done on a meat thermometer.

- Remove, slice and serve.

- Serves: 10 – 15.

Baked Pork Tenderloin

Tenderloin steaks, 1" thick (2.5 cm)	6	
GF flour mixture	½ C	125 ml
Salt	½ tsp	2 ml
Pepper	¼ tsp	1 ml
GF non-stick spray		
Onion, medium, chopped	1	
Garlic, minced	1 clove	
Ground ginger	1 tsp	5 ml
Applesauce	14 oz	398 ml
Sauterne wine (or full bodied red wine)	½ C	125 ml
Light GF soya sauce	½ C	125 ml

- Preheat oven to 350°F (180°C)
- Flatten tenderloins slightly with cleaver
- In a medium sized bowl mix together the salt, pepper and GF flour mixture
- Coat a frying pan with the non stick cooking spray
- Dip each portion of pork tenderloin in the GF flour mixture ensuring each piece is well coated, transfer to frying pan
- Brown all pieces and transfer to baking dish that has been coated with non-stick cooking spray
- Prepare applesauce mixture:
  - Over medium heat brown in a frying pan the onion until soft

- Add garlic and cook for 2 minutes, being cautious not to burn
- Add in the ginger; stir well
- Mix in the applesauce, wine and light GF soya sauce, simmer for one to two minutes, remove from stove and pour over the tenderloin
- Place in oven and bake for one hour

- Serves: 6

Beef Roast with Rub:

This recipe has evolved over time.

Beef roast (sirloin is my preference)	4 - 5 lb	1.8 – 2.3 kg
Onion, sliced	1	
Garlic, minced	3 cloves	
Dijon mustard	2 tbsp	30 ml
Paprika	1 tsp	5 ml
Oregano, dried	1 tsp	5 ml
Salt	1 tsp	2 ml
Pepper	1 tsp	2 ml
Water	1 C	500 ml

- If roast is frozen, thaw prior to preparation time

- Pre-heat oven to 350°F (180°C) degrees,

- For the rub mixture, blend in a small bowl the minced garlic, Dijon mustard, paprika, oregano, salt and pepper; stirring well to ensure well blended.

- Prepare roasting pan by adding one cup of water to the roasting pan, along with sliced onion.

- Set roast on cutting board and take rub mixture, and rub over top and sides of the roast. Do not cover bottom as it will be sitting on bottom of roaster.

- Set roaster in oven, and cook for approximately two hours, or until meat thermometer reads desired setting.

- Set meat aside for 15 minutes prior to cutting to let meat rest and juices absorb into meat.

- Slice and serve.

- Serves: 6- 8.

Notes:

➢ For a more intense flavour the water can be substituted for red wine.

➢ Serve with mashed potatoes, popovers, gravy and vegetables.

Chilli:

This recipe has evolved over time.

GF non-stick spray		
Lean ground beef	3 ½ lbs	1750 g
Green bell pepper, chopped	1 medium	
Onion, chopped	1 ½ C	375 ml
Garlic, minced	1 clove	
Chilli powder	2 tsp	10 ml
Cumin, ground	1 tsp	5 ml
Oregano, dried	1 tsp	5 ml
Salt	½ tsp	2 ml
Brown sugar, packed	1 tbsp	15 ml
Tomato paste	13 oz can	384 ml
Water	2 C	500 ml
Ketchup	½ C	125 ml
Kidney beans, not drained (2 cans)	30 ounces 796 ml	
Monterey Jack cheese, shredded	¾ C	175 ml
Corn	1 C	250 ml

- Spray large Dutch oven with GF non-stick spray.
- Over medium high heat brown lean ground beef. Once meat is browned drain off any liquid and set aside in the Dutch oven.

- Spray a frying pan with GF non-stick spray, and add onions, green bell pepper, and garlic. Sauté over medium high heat for approximately 8 minutes or until the onions are opaque. Add Chilli powder and cumin; cook for a few more minutes and stir constantly until spices have a chance to meld together. Remove from stove.

- Return large Dutch oven with meat to stovetop, to medium heat. Add onion, green pepper mixture and stir.

- Add brown sugar, oregano, salt, tomato paste, water and ketchup, and bring to a boil. Reduce heat and let simmer uncovered for approximately 45 minutes.

- Add Kidney beans, and corn, and then simmer for another 30 minutes.

- Add Monterey jack cheese, and stir until melted.

- Serves: 10 – 12.

Note:

➢ Other options for adding to the Chilli: Mushrooms, Chopped Carrots, what ever you choose.

Fondue without Oil:

A tasty and lighter version of fondue from the traditional oil based fondues.

GF Chicken broth, strong	2 C	500 ml
White wine, dry	2 C	500 ml
Onion, medium, thinly sliced	1	
Celery, chopped	2 C	500 ml
Garlic, chopped	1 clove	
Peppercorns, crushed	10	
Salt	½ tsp	2 ml
Tarragon leaves dried	1 tsp	5 ml
Parsley	½ tsp	2 ml
Thyme, dried	½ tsp	2 ml
Bay leaf	1	
A variety of Beef, Chicken, Pork, Seafood,	3 lbs	1500 g

(Served in bite size pieces – 1 inch cubes)

Fondue base:

- For maximum flavour prepare the fondue base, three days before serving.

- In a large (4 quart saucepan), combine chicken broth and wine and bring to a boil.

- Add the onion, celery, garlic, peppercorns, salt, tarragon, thyme, parsley and bay leaf. Bring to a boil again.

- Cool and then refrigerate until required.

<u>Fonduing</u>:

- When required strain the fondue base through a fine strainer and pour into a fondue pot. Bring to a boil. Ensure the burner is adjusted to ensure the mixture boils through the meal.

- Serves: 4.

<u>Note:</u>

➢ See Sauces section for selection of sauces to serve with the fondue.

Greek Ribs:

Oregano, dried	3 tbsp	45 ml
Seasoning salt	1 tbsp	15 ml
Garlic powder	1 tbsp	15 ml
Lemon pepper	1 ½ tbsp	22 ml
Pork spare ribs	3 ½ lbs	1750 g
Lemon juice	¼ C	60 ml

- Preheat oven to 350°F (180°C).
- Trim fat off of ribs, cut into small sections (finger food size).
- In a large bowl, blend together, oregano, seasoning salt, garlic powder and lemon pepper.
- Add ribs and coat evenly in the seasoning mixture.
- Place on a lightly greased or sheet of parchment paper, on a cookie sheet with sides.
- Evenly distribute coated ribs over the cookie sheet.
- Bake ribs for approximately 45 minutes, turning once. During the baking process brush ribs once with lemon juice.
- Remove and cool for approximately 5 minutes before serving.
- Serves: 5.

Layered Ground Beef and Zucchini:

Zucchini, sliced for layering	6 C	1500 ml
Ground beef	1 lb	500 g
Garlic, minced	2	
Spaghetti sauce	2 C	500 ml
Salt	½ tsp	2 ml
Oregano, dried	½ tsp	2 ml
Basil, dried	½ tsp	2 ml
Cottage cheese	2 C	500 ml
Parsley, dried	1 tbsp	15 ml
Eggs, large, lightly beaten	2	
GF non-stick spray		
GF breadcrumbs, divided	½ C	125 ml
Mozzarella cheese, shredded, divided	2 C	500 ml
Parmesan cheese, divided	½ C	125 ml

- Preheat oven to 350°F (180°C) degrees.
- Sauté the ground beef over medium high heat and drain, to ensure all fat is removed from the ground beef.
- Add garlic and sauté for 2 – 3 minutes longer.
- Add spaghetti sauce, salt, basil, oregano, and cook for an additional minute. Remove from heat.
- In a medium sized bowl blend together the cottage cheese, parsley, ¼ C (65 ml) Parmesan cheese and eggs.

- Coat a shallow 11 x 17 baking dish (28 x 43) with GF non-stick spray and begin layering half of the zucchini on the bottom of the pan.

- With half of the GF breadcrumbs, sprinkle over the first layer of zucchini then spread half of the cottage cheese mixture, then add half of the meat mixture and 1 cup (125 ml) of the mozzarella cheese; repeat the layering process of zucchini, meat, and cottage cheese mixture.

- Bake for 40 minutes.

- Top off with remaining mozzarella (1 C or 125 ml) and Parmesan cheese (1/4 or 65 ml) and bake for an additional 5 minutes or until the cheese melts and is a light golden brown.

- Serves: 10.

Mom's Sweet and Sour Pork Ribs:

Pork ribs – sliced in to rib sections	2 lbs	1000 g
GF non-stick spray		
Brown sugar, packed	1 C	250 ml
Vinegar	½ C	125 ml
Water	1 ½ C	375 ml
Pineapple juice	1 ½ C	375 ml
Dijon mustard	1 ½ tsp	7 ml
Celery salt	½ tsp	2 ml
Garlic – minced	2 cloves	
Ginger	½ tsp	2 ml
GF soya sauce	¼ C	60 ml
Tabasco or other preferred hot sauce	7 – 9 drops	
Onion, medium, finely chopped	1	

Sauce Thickening:

Cornstarch	2 tbsp	30 ml
Cold water	½ C	125 ml

- Spray frying pan with GF non-stick spray, brown ribs in the frying pan.

- While ribs are browning mix together in a large bowl: brown sugar, vinegar, water, pineapple juice, Dijon mustard, celery salt, garlic, ginger, GF soya sauce, Tabasco sauce, and onion.

- Remove ribs from frying pan and blot off any excess grease with paper towel.

- Put ribs and sauce in a large pot and let simmer for 2 – 3 hours on stove top.

- Approximately 10 minutes prior to serving mix cornstarch with cold water and stir in to rib mixture on low heat.

- Bring to a low boil and let continue to cook over low heat for 10 minutes.

- Serves: 4.

Pork Chops in Marinade:

Lime juice	1 tbsp	15 ml
Orange juice	1 tbsp	15 ml
GF soya sauce	½ C	125 ml
Ground ginger	½ tsp	2 ml
Pepper	¼ tsp	1 ml
Garlic, minced	2 cloves	
Bay leaf	1	
Honey	2 tbsp	30 ml
Cilantro (dried)	1 tsp	5 ml
Lean pork chops	6 – 8	

- Prepare marinade 30 minutes prior to use. For a more flavourful meal, marinate pork chops 24 hours prior to use.

- In a glass bowl, or self-locking plastic bag, mix together: lime juice, orange juice, GF soya sauce, ground ginger, pepper, minced garlic, bay leaf, honey and cilantro.

- Add in pork chops and coat meat with marinade. Cover and store in the fridge prior to use.

- Broil or grill until done through.

- Serves: 6.

Pork Kabobs:

Lime juice from one lime		
Vegetable oil	¼ C	60 ml
Coriander, whole crushed	¼ tsp	1 ml
Onion, chopped	¼ C	60 ml
Garlic, minced	1 clove	
Pepper	¼ tsp	1 ml
Lean pork cut into 1-inch cubes (2.5 cm)	1-¼ lbs	625 g
Zucchini, medium sized, washed sliced	1	
Red peppers, washed cut into chunks	2	
Whole mushrooms, washed and patted dry	½ lbs	250 g

- Prepare pork marinade 24 hours prior to cooking for most flavourful taste. In a glass bowl, or self-locking plastic bag, add lime juice, vegetable oil, crushed whole coriander, chopped onion, minced garlic, pepper and pork cubes. Stir or shake to coat meat with marinade.

- Cover and store in the fridge.

- If using wooden skewers soak in water for ½ hour prior to use, this will assist in helping the skewers not to burn while cooking.

- To prepare kabobs, drain pork from marinade and begin skewering meat and alternating with zucchini, red pepper, and mushroom pieces.

- Broil or grill until done through.

- Serves: 4.

Pork Stir Fry:

Italian dressing	¼ C	60 ml
Lean pork tenderloin, cut into thin strips	1 lb	500 g
Red pepper, cut into thin strips	1	
Sugar snap peas	2 C	500 ml
Green onions, diagonally sliced	¾ C	150 ml
GF soya sauce	2 tbsp	30 ml
Cornstarch	1 tsp	5 ml
Ginger, ground	½ tsp	3 ml

- Heat the Italian dressing in a large skillet on medium high heat.

- Add meat, cook and stir 2 minutes. Add peppers and peas and cook 3 minutes stirring frequently; add in green onions and cook an additional minute.

- In a small bowl blend together the GF soya sauce, cornstarch and ginger until well blended. Add to meat mixture in skillet, cook an additional minute or until sauce thickens.

- Serves: 4.

Note:
➢ Suggest serving over rice

Steak and Mushroom Kabobs:

Red wine	½ C	125 ml
Vegetable oil	½ C	125 ml
Dijon mustard	1 tsp	5 ml
Ketchup	2 tbsp	30 ml
Garlic, minced	1 clove	
Granulated sugar	1 tsp	5 ml
Salt	½ tsp	2 ml
Vinegar	1 tbsp	15 ml
Marjoram, dried	pinch	
Rosemary, dried	pinch	
Tenderloin steak cut into 1-inch cubes (2.5 cm)	1-¼ lbs	625 g
Mushrooms caps, small, washed	½ lb	250 g

- Prepare steak marinade 2 hours prior for most flavourful taste.

- In a glass bowl, or self-locking plastic bag, add red wine, vegetable oil, Dijon mustard, ketchup, minced garlic, sugar, salt, vinegar, marjoram, rosemary, and steak cubes. Stir or shake to coat meat with marinade. Cover and store in the fridge, mixing occasionally while stored in the fridge.

- If using wooden skewers soak in water for ½ hour prior to use, this will ensure skewers do no burn while cooking.

- To prepare kabobs, drain steak from the marinade and begin skewering meat and alternating with mushrooms.

- Broil or grill until done through.

- Serves: 4, (2 skewers each).

Stew with Dumplings:

Stew:

Chuck Steak,	2 lbs	1000 g
cut into 1-inch cubes (2.5 cm)		
Red wine (optional)	½ C	125 ml
GF non-stick spray		
Water	5 C	1250 ml
Onions, chopped	½ C	125 ml
Garlic, minced (optional)	1 clove	
Bay leaf	1	
Potatoes, peeled and cut into cubes	2 large	
Turnip, peeled and cut into large chunks	1 large	
Carrots, peeled and cut into cubes	2 large	
Pepper	1.2 tsp	2 ml
Salt	1 tsp	5 ml
Peas	1 C	250 ml

Thickening: (Optional if not having with dumpling recipe)

Cornstarch	3 tbsp	45 ml
Water, cool	½ C	125 ml

- Spray cast iron frying pan with GF non-stick spray (preferred for browning meat).
- Brown chuck steak pieces in a cast iron frying pan. When done transfer to large stewing pot.

- Add red wine, water, onions, garlic and bay leaf. Bring to a boil and reduce to simmer for approximately 2 hours. Stir occasionally to ensure liquid is still covering meat, if not add more water.

- After 2 hours, add potatoes, turnip, carrots, salt and pepper. Bring to a boil and reduce to simmer.

- Approximately 20 minutes prior to serving add in peas, stir. Remove bay leaf. If turnips are not an enjoyed vegetable, they can be removed at this point. They do add a nice flavour to the stew.

- Mix together the cornstarch and water mixture, and pour slowly into stew mixture, ensure constant stirring. Bring to a boil for 1 minute, reduce heat and simmer.

- Add dumplings. See dumpling recipe. Remember no peeking when dumplings are added.

- Serves: 4 - 5

- For Dumplings, see Dumpling recipe

Terry's Meat Loaf:

GF non-stick spray

Ingredient	Imperial	Metric
GF Bread crumbs	½ C	125 ml
Milk	¾ C	175 ml
Onion, finely chopped	¼ C	60 ml
Garlic clove, minced	1	
Parsley, dried	2 tbsp	30 ml
Ketchup	3 tbsp	45 ml
Dijon Mustard	1 tbsp	15 ml
Sage	½ tsp	2 ml
Ground beef, lean	1 ½ lbs	750 g
Eggs, large, beaten	2	
Salt	2 tsp	10 ml
Black pepper	1 tsp	5ml
Brown sugar	2 tbsp	30 ml

- Heat oven to 350°F (180°C).
- Coat a loaf pan with GF non-stick spray.
- In large mixing bowl add eggs and beat slightly.
- Add milk, breadcrumbs, onion, parsley, salt, sage, pepper, minced garlic and stir together.
- Add ground beef and mix well.
- Place mixture into the greased loaf pan. Bake for 75 minutes.
- In small mixing bowl stir together the ketchup, brown sugar and Dijon mustard and set aside.

- Remove meatloaf from oven, drain any excess fat, and then cover the meatloaf with the above mixture and return to oven for 10 minutes.

Meat thermometer inserted into the center of the loaf registers 160°F (70°C). Let meat loaf cool for approximately 5 minutes before serving. Serves: 6.

Chicken

Chicken in Apricot Sauce:

GF Russian dressing	1 Bottle	250 ml
Apricot Jam	1 Jar	450 ml
GF Onion Soup mix	1 pkg	
Chicken Breasts	6 pieces	

- Preheat oven to 350°F (180°C) degrees.
- In a bowl mix together the Russian dressing, apricot jam, and onion soup mix.
- Rinse off the chicken pieces or parts, pat dry, and place in a greased baking dish.
- Pour jam and Russian dressing mixture over chicken.
- Bake for 1 hour or until done.
- Serves: 4 – 6.

Chicken Kiev:

GF non-stick spray

Chicken breasts (already de-boned)	4	
Eggs, large	2	
GF Breadcrumbs	1 C	250 ml
GF flour mixture	½ C	125 ml
Parmesan cheese	¼ C	50 ml

Garlic Butter - Filling

Garlic cloves, minced	6 cloves	
Butter, softened	5 oz	125 ml
Parsley, chopped	1 tbsp	15 ml
Salt	to taste	
Pepper	to taste	

- Preheat oven to 350°F (180°C) degrees.
- Prepare garlic butter by mixing the softened butter with the minced garlic and parsley, and season with the salt and pepper.
- Spray 9 x 9 (22 x 22 cm) baking dish with GF non-stick spray.
- Slice a pocket into the chicken breast, being careful not to cut through the breast.
- Pipe into each pocket on the chicken the garlic butter filling.
- Place chicken in the freezer for one hour, this helps the garlic butter to remain in the pocket when baking.

- Mix together the breadcrumbs and Parmesan cheese.

- Dredge the chicken breast into the GF flour mixture and then dip into the egg mixture and roll in GF breadcrumb mixture.

- Bake for 1 hour.

- Serves: 4.

Chicken Parmesan:

GF non-stick spray		
Chicken breasts	4	
Eggs, large	3	
GF Breadcrumbs	1 C	250 ml
Parmesan cheese	3 tbsp	45 ml
Tomato sauce	14 oz	398 ml
Mozzarella cheese	½ C	125 ml
Parmesan cheese	¼ C	50 ml
Salt	to taste	
Pepper	to taste	

- Preheat oven to 350°F (180°C) degrees.
- In a medium sized bowl mix the GF breadcrumbs with 3 tbsp of the Parmesan cheese, add in the salt and pepper and mix well.
- In separate medium sized bowl beat the eggs.
- Prepare a non-stick frying pan by heating up to medium to medium-high temperature on stove top.
- Dip pieces of chicken breasts in the beaten egg mixture and roll in GF breadcrumb mixture.
- Place in non-stick frying pan and brown on both sides to a golden brown color.
- Place pieces in a baking dish and cover with tomato sauce.

- Sprinkle with remaining Parmesan cheese and all the mozzarella cheese.

- Bake for 1 hour.

- Serves: 4.

Chicken in Red Wine Sauce:

GF flour mixture	½ C	125 ml
Green onions – chopped	3	
Mushrooms, medium, sliced	10	
Chicken Breasts	4 breasts	
Butter	1 tbsp	15 ml
Red wine	½ C	125 ml
Chicken base	2 tbsp	30 ml
Pepper	to taste	
Water	½ C	125 ml
Cornstarch	2 tbsp	30 ml

- Prepare a non-stick frying pan by heating up to medium to medium-high temperature on stove top.

- Dip chicken in GF flour mixture and pan fry.

- When the chicken is brown on both sides add mushrooms and green onions.

- Mix in red wine and half of the water along with the chicken base and pepper.

- Mix together the remaining water and 2 tbsp of cornstarch and then pour into pan to make sauce for chicken mixture. Reduce heat and bring to a low boil for approximately 10 minutes.

- Serves: 4.

Crunchy Parmesan Chicken:

GF non-stick spray

Chicken, parts of or breasts	1	
If breasts, halved and de boned	6 halves	
Eggs, large	2	
Parmesan cheese	1/3 C	75 ml
GF flour mixture	½ C	125 ml
Cayenne pepper	¼ tsp	1 ml
Salt	1 ½ tsp	7 ml
Fresh ground pepper (to taste)		
Sweet paprika	1 ¼ tsp	6 ml
Thyme, dried	1 ½ tsp	7 ml

- Preheat oven to 375°F (190°C) degrees.

- Rinse chicken and pat dry with paper towels; remove skin and cut away excess fat.

- In a shallow, medium bowl, combine Parmesan cheese, GF flour mixture, salt, thyme, cayenne pepper, paprika, and fresh ground pepper.

- Beat eggs.

- Spray baking dish with GF non-stick spray.

- Dip pieces of chicken in egg mixture and roll in Parmesan/ spice mixture. Ensure chicken is well coated, and place in baking dish.

- Bake, basting with the pan juices occasionally, tilting the pan to obtain the juices from the corners.

- Bake for 1 hour.

- Serves: 4.

Garlic Roasted Chicken:

Roasting chicken	5 – 6 lbs	2.5 kgs
Water	½ C	125 ml
Garlic cloves, peeled	8 - 10	
Whole heads of garlic	2	
Olive oil	2 tbsp	30 ml
Salt	to taste	
Pepper	to taste	

- Preheat oven to 450° F (230°C) degrees.

- Clean chicken by removing giblets and neck; rinse with cold water and pat chicken dry. Remove any excess fat from the chicken.

- Loosening the skin in the area of the breast and randomly insert garlic cloves on chicken breasts, legs and in cavity area.

- Place chicken in roasting pan, breast side up and bake for 30 minutes at 450 F.

- Place water in bottom of roasting pan, and sprinkle salt and pepper over chicken. After cooking chicken for 30 minutes at 450° F (230°C), reduce oven temperature to 350°F (180°C), chicken will require two of baking time; check chicken with meat thermometer to reduce doubt if done.

- Cut tops off of garlic, leaving the roots intact.

- Brush garlic heads with olive oil and arrange around chicken and reduce temperature to 350°F (180°C).

- When done, remove garlic heads and serve with crackers or small pieces of GF bread – toasted, or use as a side item when presenting the carved chicken.

- Serves: 6 – 8

Note:

➢ Serving suggestion – serve with GF Bread Stuffing or Potato Stuffing and Chicken Gravy.

Herb Roasted Chicken:

Roasting Chicken	5 – 6 lbs	2.5 kgs
Basil, dried	1 tsp	5 ml
Thyme, dried	1 tsp	5 ml
Rosemary, dried and crushed	½ tsp	2 ml
Salt	½ tsp	2 ml
Black pepper	¼ tsp	1 ml

- Preheat oven to 375°F (190°C).

- Rinse chicken with cold water; pat dry. Trim excess fat. Loosen skin from thigh and leg by inserting fingers, gently pushing between skin and meat.

- Combine basil, thyme, rosemary, salt and pepper.

- Rub herb mixture under loosened skin.

- Place chicken on a broiler pan. Insert meat thermometer into meaty part of thigh, making sure not to touch bone.

- Bake at 375°F (190°C).for 45 minutes. Increase oven temperature to 450°F (230°C), (do not remove chicken from oven).

- Bake 30 minutes or until thermometer registers 180°F (90°C). Cover chicken loosely with foil; let stand 10 minutes. Discard skin.

- Serves: 5 - 7.

Lemon Garlic Chicken with Homemade BBQ Sauce:

GF non-stick spray		
Chicken-breast halves, skinned, de-boned	8	
Lemon juice	1/3 C	75 ml
Dijon mustard	3 tbsp	45 ml
Garlic powder	1/2 tsp	2 ml
Mayonnaise, light	2 tbsp	30 ml
BBQ sauce	2 tbsp	30 ml
Paprika	¼ tsp	1 ml
Chilli powder	1 tsp	5 ml
Breadcrumbs	¾ C	175 ml
Parmesan cheese	¼ C	65 ml

- Preheat oven to 400°F (200°C).

- Combine lemon juice, Dijon mustard and garlic powder in a large glass bowl or re-sealable plastic bag for marinating chicken; reserve 2 tablespoons for the homemade BBQ sauce in a small bowl.

- Add chicken to the lemon juice mixture, turning to coat, and let marinate for approximately 30 minutes.

- In the small bowl with the reserved 2 tablespoons of lemon juice mixture add: mayonnaise, barbeque sauce, Chilli powder, and paprika. Cover and chill.

- Spray broiler pan with GF non-stick spray.

- Mix together breadcrumbs and Parmesan cheese in a bowl for dredging chicken.

- Remove chicken breasts from the marinade; discard remainder of marinade.

- Dredge chicken in the breadcrumb mixture and place on broiler pan.

- Bake for 45 minutes or until golden brown and chicken is done.

- Serves: 6 –8, with 2 tablespoons of homemade BBQ sauce each.

Lettuce Wraps with Chicken:

Chicken breasts, thinly sliced	3	
Garlic clove, finely minced	1	
Carrots, thinly sliced	½ C	125 ml
Red Pepper, medium in size, thinly sliced	1	
Head lettuce, large leaves	8 – 10 large leaves	

- Use a large non-stick frying pan; add in minced garlic and sauté garlic for 2 – 3 minutes, being careful not to burn the garlic.

- Add chicken slices, and cook until chicken is done.

- Add in vegetables and sauté until tender but not soft.

- Rinse off head lettuce, and dry off, retaining the large leaves. Use the lettuce leaves as a wrap for the chicken mixture.

- Serves: 4 (2 per person).

Options:

Vegetables can vary depending upon personal preference, some suggestions:

Water chestnuts, drained; bamboo shoots, drained; yellow peppers.

Note:
➢ Suggested Sauces for Chicken Wraps: (See Sauce section for more ideas)
  - Teriyaki Sauce
  - Peanut Sauce

Pineapple Chicken:

GF non-stick spray

Chicken Parts	3 lbs	1500 g

Salt (to taste)

Pepper (to taste)

- Use a large non-stick frying pan on medium to medium high heat.
- Add chicken parts and brown on both sides; sprinkle with salt and pepper.
- Transfer to small roasting pan.

Pineapple Sauce:

Pineapple pieces, reserve juice	1 can	398 ml
Water	1 C	250 ml
White vinegar	¼ C	60 ml
Brown sugar, packed	¼ C	60 ml
GF soya sauce	1 tbsp	15 ml
Salt	½ tsp	2 ml
Cornstarch	1 tbsp	15 ml
Green pepper, seeded and cut in strips	1	

- Preheat oven to 350°F (180°C) degrees.

- In a large frying pay mix together the pineapple juice, water, white vinegar, packed brown sugar, GF soya sauce, salt and cornstarch.

- Heat and stir until the mixture boils and thickens slightly.

- Stir in pineapple and green pepper, cooking for another 2 – 3 minutes.

- Pour over top of chicken in roasting pan and bake covered for approximately 1.5 hours or until tender.

- Serves: 4 – 6.

Szechwan Chicken (Kang Pao Chicken):

Chicken-breast halves, skinned, de-boned	4	
(Cut into approximately ¾ inch/2 cm cubes)		
Egg white	1	
Corn starch	1 tbsp	15 ml
Vegetable oil	2 tbsp	30 ml
Unsalted peanuts or cashews	1 C	250 ml
Green onions, sliced	2	
Dry sherry	2 tbsp	30 ml
Hoisin sauce	2 tbsp	30 ml
Black bean sauce	4 tbsp	60 ml
Chilli paste	¼ tsp	1 ml
Vinegar	1 tbsp	15 ml
Granulated sugar	1tsp	5 ml

- In a medium sized bowl, combine the cubed chicken with the egg white and cornstarch.

- Refrigerate for 1/2 hour.

- Heat oil in wok and stir-fry chicken 3 to 4 minutes, until done.

- Add nuts, green onions, dry sherry, hoisin sauce, black bean sauce, chilli paste vinegar, and granulated sugar to the wok; stirring often to ensure ingredients are well mixed.

- Heat thoroughly and serve at once with rice, or with rice noodles.

- Serves: 4.

<u>Note:</u>

➢ If you do not have a wok, you can use a large frying pan.

Sauces and Salsas

Fruit Salsa:

Strawberries, chopped	1 ½ C	
Mango, chopped peeled	¾ C	
Mint, fresh, chopped	1 tsp	5 ml
Pepper, coarsely ground	½ tsp	2 ml

- Combine all ingredients in a small bowl, cover and chill.
- Makes 3 cups (750 ml), each serving size is ½ C (125 ml).

<u>Note:</u>

➢ A nice side dish to serve with a baked chicken breast.

Fondue Sauces:

Horseradish Cream Sauce:

Light sour cream	½ C	125 ml
Dijon mustard	1 tsp	5 ml
Horseradish	3 tbsp	45 ml
Paprika	½ tsp	2 ml

- Gently fold together sour cream, Dijon mustard, horseradish, and paprika.

- Refrigerate until required.

Seafood Cocktail Sauce:

Ketchup	¾ C	175 ml
Horseradish	2 tbsp	30 ml
Lemon juice	2 tbsp	30 ml
Salt	½ tsp	2 ml
Hot pepper sauce	¼ tsp	1 ml

- In a small bowl blend together ketchup, horseradish, lemon juice, salt and hot pepper sauce.

- Refrigerate until required in an airtight container for up to three days.

Teriyaki Sauce:

GF soya sauce	¼ C	60 ml
Dry sherry	¼ C	60 ml
(Substitute: Japanese rice wine – sake)		
Granulated sugar	2 tbsp	30 ml
Garlic,	2 cloves	
Ginger,	1 tbsp	15 ml
(Ginger if dried)	1 tsp	5 ml
Pepper	½ tsp	2 ml

- In a small saucepan combine GF soya sauce, dry sherry, sugar, garlic, ginger and pepper.

- Bring to a boil over medium heat, stirring occasionally.

Note:

➢ If the preference is to have a thicker sauce, this mixture can be thickened using cornstarch. Remember to mix the cornstarch (1 tbsp/15 ml) with a ¼ C (60 ml) of cool liquid prior to adding to the hot mixture. Stir mixture more frequently, lower heat and cook for another 2 – 3 minutes.

Gravy - Beef:

Cornstarch	3 tbsp	45 ml
Roast drippings, degreased or beef broth	1 1/2 C	375 ml
Water	½ C	125 ml
Red wine, dry	½ C	125 ml
Salt	to taste	
Black pepper	to taste	

- In a small bowl add cornstarch and gradually add half of the water and stir well.

- In a medium saucepan, or the pan the roast was in, add the remaining water and red wine.

- Bring this mixture to a boil and add the cornstarch mixture.

- Reduce heat to a slow boil and cook for another 5 minutes.

- Remove from heat and add salt and pepper to taste.

Gravy - Chicken:

Cornstarch	3 tbsp	45 ml
Chicken drippings, degreased or chicken broth	1 1/2 C	375 ml
Water	½ C	125 ml
White wine, dry	½ C	125 ml
Salt	to taste	
Black pepper	to taste	

- In a small bowl add cornstarch and gradually add half of the water and stir well.

- In a medium saucepan, or the pan the chicken was in, add the remaining water and white wine.

- Bring this mixture to a boil and add the cornstarch mixture.

- Reduce heat to a slow boil and cook for another 5 minutes.

- Remove from heat and add salt and pepper to taste.

Mango Salsa:

Mango, peeled and chopped	1 C	250 ml
Red pepper, chopped	1/3 C	75 ml
Cilantro, dried	1 tbsp	15 ml
Balsamic or white wine vinegar	1 tbsp	15 ml

- Mix together above ingredients, let sit for 1 hour prior to serving.
- Makes approximately 1 1/3 C (325 ml) of salsa

Note:

➢ Nice addition to a complement a baked chicken breast or a smoked turkey.

Peanut Sauce:

GF Smooth or chunky peanut butter	¼ C	60 ml
GF soya sauce	¼ C	60 ml
Milk	¼ C	60 ml
Granulated sugar	½ tsp	2 ml
Garlic – minced	2 cloves	
Chillies	¼ - ½ tsp	1 - 2 ml
(Add more if you like zesty sauce)		
Cornstarch	1 tbsp	15 ml
Water	½ C	125 ml

- Using either a medium sized bowl add the peanut butter, GF soya sauce, milk, sugar and garlic.

- Gradually add a quarter cup of the water and stir until well blended.

- Add chillies and let sit for 1 hour to permit the flavours to blend.

- Transfer mixture to a dish suitable for the microwave, heat mixture for approximately one - two minutes in the microwave on full power.

- Mix together cornstarch and remaining quarter cup of water, pour into the warm peanut mixture and stir well. Return the mixture to the microwave and heat for another minute.

- Makes approximately 3/4 C (175 ml) of peanut sauce.

<u>Notes:</u>

➢ There are two options for cooking the peanut sauce; both need to be watched so that the mixture does not burn.

➢ If cooking the peanut sauce on the stovetop, cook on medium to low – stirring constantly.

➢ For the microwave be cautious of the strength of your microwave, check every minute to ensure sauce does not burn.

➢ If the mixture sits longer prior to being cooked the sauce will be zestier.

Pineapple Sauce:

Crushed pineapple with juice	14 oz	398 ml
Granulated sugar	1 C	250 ml
Water	1 C	250 ml
Lemon juice	2 tbsp	30 ml
Cornstarch	2 tbsp	30 ml

- Measure all ingredients into a medium size saucepan.

- Heat and stir until mixture comes to a boil and thickens, approximately 3 – 5 minutes.

- Makes approximately: 3 C (700 ml) of pineapple sauce.

Note:

➢ This sauce is quite versatile. It can be made ahead of time, covered, and refrigerated. You can serve it cold or at room temperature, or reheat it.

➢ The sauce can be served as a topping on ice cream, cheese cake, or served warm over a roasted chicken breast or baked chicken pieces.

Pizza Sauce

Tomato paste	1 6oz can	170 g
Water, use tomato paste can as measure	1 can	
Oregano	½ tsp	2 ml
Basil leaves	1 tsp	5 ml
Salt	1 tsp	5 ml
Pepper	¼ tsp	1 ml
Onion, minced	¼ C	
Garlic, minced	1 clove	

- In a medium sized bowl, blend together tomato paste and water.
- Add to the mixture, oregano, basil leaves, salt, pepper, onion, and garlic.

Raspberry Sauce:

Frozen raspberries in syrup,	10 oz	307 g
(Thawed and un-drained)		
Water	2 tbsp	30 ml
Cornstarch	2 tsp	10 ml

- Drain raspberries, reserving syrup. Press raspberries through a sieve into a bowl, reserving purée; discard seeds.

- Combine water and cornstarch in a saucepan; stir until blended. Stir in reserved raspberry syrup and purée; bring to a boil, and cook 1 minute, stirring constantly. Pour into a bowl; cool.

- Serves: 3/4 cup (serving size: 2 tablespoons)

Note:

➤ This sauce is quite versatile. It can be made ahead of time, covered, and refrigerated. You can serve it cold or at room temperature, or reheat it.

➤ The sauce can be served as a topping on ice cream, cheese cake, or served warm over a roasted chicken breast or baked pork chops.

Sweet and Sour Sauce:

Brown sugar, packed	2 C	500 ml
Cornstarch	2 tbsp	30 ml
Water	1/3 C	75 ml
Vinegar	½ C	125 ml
GF soya sauce	2 tbsp	30 ml
Ketchup	2 tbsp	30 ml

- Measure all ingredients into a medium size saucepan.
- Heat and stir until mixture comes to a boil and thickens.
- Serves: 3/4 C (175 ml)

Fish and Seafood

Pan-Fried Garlic-Scallop Dumplings:

Scallops, minced	½ lb	250 g
Green onion	¼ C	60 ml
GF soya sauce	2 tbsp	30 ml
Ginger, fresh minced	1 tbsp	15 ml
Chilli oil	½ tsp	2 ml
Garlic, minced	4	
Vegetable oil, divided	2 tsp	10 ml
Water	½ C	125 ml
Rice paper wrappers	36	

- Combine scallops, green onions, GF soya sauce, ginger, Chilli oil, and garlic.

- In a medium saucepan, fill half full of water and bring to a boil and then reduce to a simmer.

- Using thongs, dip one rice paper wrapper at a time. Then spoon in about 1 ½ tsp of scallop mixture into the center of each rice paper wrapper. Fold in sides of wrapper.

- On a lightly greased cookie sheet place the completed wrapper, and cover with a damp cloth to keep them from drying.

- Repeat these steps until all the scallop mixture has been used.

- Prepare double boiler with a steamer top, boil water and reduce to medium heat.

- In a large non-stick frying pan heat 1 tsp of oil over medium-high heat.

- Arrange half of the dumplings in the skillet; cover and cook 5 minutes or until lightly brown.

- Place the browned dumplings on the steamer, cover and steam for 5 minutes. Remove dumplings and keep warm.

- Repeat cooking procedure with remaining dumplings.

- Serve with GF soya sauce for dipping sauce.

- Serves: 36 dumplings.

Salmon Poached with a Simple White Sauce:

Salmon fillet	1 lb	500g
Water	3 C	750 ml
Lemon, small thinly sliced	1	
GF Chicken bouillon	2 tsp	10 ml
Mayonnaise	3 tbsp	45 ml
Dill, dried	1 tsp	5 ml
Milk	1 tbsp	15 ml
Pickle juice	2 tsp	10 ml
Dijon mustard	1 ½ tsp	7 ml
Grated lemon rind	¼ tsp	1 ml
Lemon juice	¼ tsp	1 ml

- To prepare the salmon, cut fillet into 4 pieces. In a large skillet, bring the 3 cups of water to a boil. Once boiling, add the lemon slices and chicken bouillon. Cover and let simmer for 5 minutes, for flavour infusion.

- Place salmon pieces in to the skillet of water and raise temperature to bring it back to a boil. Reduce heat to low and cover and simmer for 8 – 10 minutes. Fish is done when it flakes easily when tested with the fork.

- For white sauce, in a small bowl mix together mayonnaise, dill, milk, pickle juice, Dijon mustard, lemon rind and lemon juice. Set aside in fridge until required.

- Pour the white sauce over salmon fillets prior to serving.

- Yield: 4 servings

<u>Note:</u>

➢ A nice addition to this dish is serving it on a bed of rice and a side of vegetables like: julienne carrots, thinly sliced zucchini, or asparagus.

Teriyaki Salmon

Salmon steaks or fillets	4	

Marinade:

GF soya sauce	¼ C	60 ml
Dry sherry	¼ C	60 ml
(Substitute: Japanese rice wine – sake)		
Granulated sugar	2 tbsp	30 ml
Garlic – minced	2 cloves	
Ginger, fresh	1 tbsp	15 ml
Pepper	½ tsp	2 ml

- In large shallow non-metallic dish with cover or large plastic bag, combine GF soya sauce, dry sherry, sugar, garlic, ginger root and pepper.

- Let salmon steaks marinade in above mixture for 30 minutes at room temperature or for up to 2 hours in the fridge, turning occasionally.

- Transfer marinade to a small sauce pan,

- Put salmon steaks on greased broiler rack, and broil approximately 4 inches (10 cm) on medium high heat. Cooking time is approximately 10 minutes per inch (2.5 cm) thickness, turning once and brushing with remaining marinade in saucepan. Fish flakes easily when cooked.

- Bring remainder of marinade to a boil over high heat for approximately 3 minutes, stirring occasionally.

- Serves: 4

Pastas and Pizzas

Lasagna:

Ingredient	Amount	Metric
GF lasagna noodles, cooked	12	
Garlic, minced	1 clove	
Ground beef, lean	1 lb	500 g
GF non-stick spray		
Onion, medium, chopped,	1	
Freshly ground pepper	½ tsp	2 ml
Salt	½ tsp	2 ml
Shredded cheeses		
Cheddar	1 C	250 ml
Mozzarella	2 C	500 ml
Parmesan cheese	½ C	125 ml
Tomato sauce/Spaghetti sauce	16 oz jar	500 ml
Cottage cheese	2 C	500 ml

- Preheat oven to 350°F (180°C).
- Cook pasta in boiling salted water just until tender (8 - 10 minutes) Drain well and set aside.
- Spray frying pan with GF non-stick spray to prevent sticking, and sauté onion, then add garlic and cook for an additional 2 – 3 minutes, be careful not to burn the garlic, and set aside.
- Brown the ground beef and drain fat.
- Add onion and garlic to ground beef mixture.
- In another bowl, blend together the salt, freshly ground pepper, cottage cheese and Parmesan cheese.

- Spray a 9 x 13 x 1 ¾ inch (34 x 23 x 4 cm) shallow baking dish with GF non-stick spray.

- To begin assembling the dish, start with spreading some tomato/spaghetti sauce on the bottom of the dish, add a layer of noodles to cover the sauce, then cover with the following items:

  Spread out half of the cottage cheese mixture

  Cover with a quarter of the cheddar and mozzarella cheese

  Cover with half of the ground beef mixture

  Cover again with tomato/spaghetti sauce

  Apply another layer,

  Top off with remaining noodles and cover with remaining cheese

- Bake for ½ hour, and until cheese is a melted and edges are bubbling.

- Serves: 8.

Linguine in a White Clam Sauce:

GF linguine noodles	1 lbs	454 g
(rice or corn flour noodles)		
Butter	4 tbsp	60 ml
Clams, minced	10 ounces	284 ml
Green onions, chopped	8	
Garlic clove, minced	2	
Cornstarch	2 tbsp	30 ml
White wine, dry	½ C	125 ml
Hot water	¾ C	225 ml
Whipping cream	1 C	225 ml
Salt	to taste	
Pepper, ground	to taste	
Parmesan cheese	½ C	125 ml
Parsley, dried or fresh chopped	½ tsp	2 ml

- Cook the rice or corn flour pasta in boiling salted water just until tender (6 – 8 minutes) Drain into a large bowl and set aside.

- Melt butter in heavy bottom frying pan.

- Sauté onions green onions until tender add in garlic and continue cooking until garlic is slightly browned; being careful not to burn the garlic.

- Drain liquid from clams, and pour into a medium bowl, add cornstarch and stir to ensure cornstarch is well mixed; this will create a thickening of the sauce when added.

- Add cream to the onion, garlic mixture and continue cooking over medium heat.

- Add clam mixture and mix thoroughly in the cream mixture.

- Add the white wine, and hot water and mix to develop a nice thick sauce.

- Add parmesan cheese, salt and pepper, and stir until cheese is blended in to cream and clam mixture.

- Stir in linguini into the clam mixture, ensuring linguini is well coated.

- Top with parsley and serve.

- Serves: 4.

Pizza Crust

VG

note:
doubled =
1x broiler pan
pizza

Milk	1/3 C	60 ml
Eggs, large	2	
Salt	1 tsp	5 ml
GF flour mixture	1 ¼ C	560 ml
GF baking powder	½ tsp	2 ml
Xanthan gum	1 tsp	5 ml
Canola oil	1 tbsp	15 ml

- Preheat oven to 350°F (180°C).

- In a large bowl, whisk together the eggs, canola oil and milk.

- Add to the milk mixture, salt, GF flour mixture, GF baking powder, and xanthan gum. Stir until well blended.

- As the dough will be tacky, spread GF flour mixture on the parchment paper and rollout pizza dough, when close to desired shape remove and spread on a round pizza pan.

- May need to coat your hands with GF flour to assist you spread out the dough to keep it from sticking to your hands.

- Bake pizza crust for 10 minutes, prior to putting on sauce and other fixings.

Pizza:

Pizza sauce	3/4 C	175 ml
Desired topping(s)		
Mozzarella cheese, shredded	1 C	250 ml

see recipe pg 102

119

- Preheat oven to 350°F (180°C).

- Cover pizza crust with pizza sauce

- Add your desired topping(s), and shredded mozzarella cheese. Below are some suggestions.

- Bake for 15 minutes or until cheese is melted and lightly browned.

Topping Ideas:

Chopped Ham	Pineapple chunks
Green pepper	Mushrooms
Pepperoni	Salami
Hamburger (ground beef cooked)	
Onions	Canadian bacon
Cheddar cheese	Mozzarella

Quick and Easy Macaroni:

Corn macaroni, elbow shaped	8 oz	250 g
Butter	2 tbsp	30 ml
Onion, chopped	1	
Cornstarch	1 tbsp	5 ml
Milk	1 ¼ C	310 ml
Freshly ground pepper	½ tsp	2 ml
Salt	½ tsp	2 ml
Nutmeg	¼ tsp	1 ml
Garlic, minced	1 clove	
Shredded cheese, medium or old	2 C	500 ml
Fresh chopped parsley	1 tbsp	15 ml

(1 tsp if dried)

- Cook pasta in boiling salted water just until tender (8 - 10 minutes) Drain well and set aside.
- Melt butter in ovenproof deep frying pan, medium heat.
- Add onion and cook, stirring often, until golden brown (5 - 7 minutes).
- Stir in garlic, sauté for another 1 - 2 minutes; be careful not to burn the garlic.
- Mix the cornstarch the milk, add to the butter, onion, garlic mixture and cook for 2 – 3 minutes, stir constantly as so not to burn to bottom of the pan.
- Stir in pepper, salt, and nutmeg.
- Bring to a boil, stirring constantly.

- Begin adding ¾ of grated cheese, stirring until mixture is smooth and cheese has melted.

- Remove from heat.

- Stir in pasta until coated with sauce.

- Sprinkle with remaining cheese and parsley.

- Place under broiler for approximately 3 minutes, until cheese is brown and bubbly.

- Serves: 4.

Note:

➢ Some other ideas to add variety to this dish are:

  ➢ Add in steamed broccoli.

  ➢ Add in cooked ground beef or sautéed chicken pieces.

Thai Chicken Pizza:

Pizza dough recipe		
Peanut sauce recipe		
Chicken breast, julienne	1	
Red pepper, julienne	1	
Carrot, medium sized, julienne	1	
Bean sprouts, rinsed well and patted dry	1 C	250 ml
Mozzarella cheese, if desired	½ C	125 ml

- Preheat oven to 350°F (180°C).
- Make pizza dough recipe.
- Make peanut sauce recipe.
- Sauté chicken over medium to high heat, in a non-stick frying pan until cooked through, approximately 7 minutes.
- Cook pizza dough for 10 minutes, remove from oven.
- Cover partially cooked pizza crust with the peanut sauce.
- Cover with cooked chicken, red pepper, carrot and bean sprouts.
- Top with mozzarella cheese.
- Bake for 15 minutes or until cheese is melted and lightly browned
- Serves: 4.

Salads and Dressings

Balsamic Dressing

Balsamic vinegar	¼ C	60 ml
Green onions, chopped	¼ C	60 ml
Parsley, dried	2 tsp	10 ml
Tarragon, dried	1 tsp	5 ml
Dijon mustard	2 tbsp	30 ml
Olive oil	1 ½ tbsp	20 ml
Water	1 tbsp	15 ml
Pepper	1/2 tsp	2 ml
Garlic, minced	3 cloves	

- Combine all ingredients in a bowl and stir well. Or mix in a food processor for a finer textured dressing.
- Yield: ¾ C (serving size: 3 tbsp)

Note:

➢ Suggest serving this dressing over a Tossed Salad.

Broccoli Salad:

Dressing:

Mayonnaise	1 C	250 ml
Granulated sugar	2 tbsp	30 ml
Vinegar	¼ C	60 ml

- Stir mayonnaise, sugar and vinegar together.
- Set aside.

Salad:

Broccoli	1 bunch	
Red onion, chopped	1 small	
Raisins	½ C	125 ml
Bacon	3 slices	

- Rinse and cut broccoli into bite size pieces.
- Rinse raisins and set aside with chopped red onion.
- Cook 3 strips of bacon until crispy, remove from pan, drain excess grease, cool and then crumble.
- In a medium bow, combine the broccoli, red onion, raisins and bacon together.

- Pour the dressing over the broccoli mixture and stir so all the broccoli is covered in the dressing.

- Refrigerate and stir periodically for a minimum of 1 hour before serving so the dressing can marinate with the broccoli mixture.

- Serves: 4 – 6.

Caesar Salad and Dressing:

Dressing:

Red wine vinegar	¼ C	60 ml
Balsamic vinegar	1 tsp	5 ml
Olive oil	½ C	175 ml
Dijon mustard	2 tsp	10 ml
Salt	¼ tsp	1 ml
Pepper	1/8 tsp	.5 ml
Garlic – minced	3 cloves	
Hot sauce (Tabasco)	2 – 4 drops	

- With the exception of the oil, mix all other ingredients in the blender.
- Once all ingredients are well mixed, slowly add the olive oil in a slow steady stream with the blender in operation.

Salad:

Romaine lettuce, medium, washed	1 head	
Bacon bits	¼ C	60 ml
Parmesan cheese	to taste	
Mozzarella cheese, part skimmed,	¼ C	60 ml shredded

- In a large bowl, tear the romaine lettuce leaves.
- Add in bacon bits, Parmesan and mozzarella cheeses.
- Pour over mixture in bowl and toss.

- If the salad dressing is not to be added to the salad immediately, store in fridge. It is best if the salad is made up just before the meal is to be served, otherwise the lettuce begins to go limp if made to far ahead of time.

- Serves: 6

Greek Salad

Dressing:

Canola oil or olive oil	¼ C	60 ml
Red wine vinegar	¼ C	60 ml
Water	2 tbsp	30 ml
Garlic minced	1 – 2 cloves	
Greek seasonings	2 tbsp	30 ml
Granulated sugar	1 tbsp	15 ml
Salt	¼ tsp	2 ml
Pepper	to taste	

- Put all ingredients in a small jar and shake well to mix ingredients.

Salad:

Leaf lettuce, shredded	3 C	750 ml
Feta cheese, crumbled	½. C	125 ml
Tomatoes, chopped	¼ C	60 ml
Red pepper	¼ C	60 ml
Cucumber	¼ C	60 ml

- Pour over salad just before serving, and mix well.

Orange Vinaigrette Salad:

Vinaigrette:

Orange juice concentrate (thawed)	¼ C	60 ml
Water	¼ C	60 ml
Red wine vinegar	3 tbsp	45 ml
Lemon juice	2 tbsp	30 ml
Garlic, minced	1 clove	
Granulated sugar	½ tsp	2 ml
Salt	¼ tsp	1 ml
Dijon mustard	¼ tsp	1 ml
Ginger – ground	¼ tsp	1 ml
Olive oil	¼ C	60 ml

- Combine the first nine ingredients in a container with a tight fitting lid and shake well,
- Add olive oil and shake again,
- Refrigerate for up to two weeks,
- Serves: 1 cup

Salad:

Romaine lettuce – torn	5 C	1250 ml
Mandarin orange slices	½ C	125 ml
Toasted slivered almonds	¼ C	60 ml
Red onion – chopped	¼ C	60 ml

133

- In a large salad bowl, combine the romaine lettuce, mandarin orange slices, toasted slivered almonds, and the red onion,

- Toss with ½ C (125 ml) of orange vinaigrette dressing,

- Serves: 6.

Note:

➢ To toast slivered almonds, pre-heat oven to 350°F (180°C) degrees, place slivered almonds on an ungreased shallow cookie sheet and place in oven. After 3 - 5 minutes stir over the almonds, and continue cooking for approximately 5 minutes or until the almonds are golden brown. These can be made ahead of time and stored in an air tight container for approximately 1 month.

Potato Salad:

Ingredient	Amount	Metric
Potatoes, peeled and cubed	6 – 8 medium	
Salt, used in boiling of potatoes	¼ tsp	1 ml
Eggs, large	6	
Green onions, chopped	3	
Radishes, sliced	4	
Mayonnaise	½ C	125 ml
Sour cream, light	¼ C	60 ml
Prepared mustard	2 tsp	4 ml
Vinegar	1 tbsp	15 ml
Milk	2 tbsp	30 ml
White Pepper	½ tsp	2 ml
Salt	pinch	
Celery Salt	¼ tsp	2 ml

- Wash and peel potatoes, and cut into cubes

- Boil potatoes until done, tender to the touch of a fork

- Boil eggs, when cooling eggs rinse immediately with cool water and let sit in cool water this makes it easier to peel the eggs. Chop up 5 of the eggs, and save the last one for decorating the dish.

- In a separate small mixing bowl add in mayonnaise, prepared mustard vinegar, milk, white pepper, salt and celery salt. Let sit until potato mixture is ready.

- For the potato mixture, in a mixing bowl add cooked chopped potatoes, eggs, green onions, and radishes, stir together.

- Pour over potato mixture half of the sauce and blend together, repeat until all the sauce has covered the potato mixture.

- Slice the last egg and garnish the potato mixture.

- If not serving immediately, cover and place in the refrigerator until required.

- Serves: 8.

Raspberry Vinaigrette with Spinach Salad:

Dressing:

Raspberry vinegar	2 C	500 ml
(Or red wine vinegar)		
Vegetable oil	2/3 C	150 ml
Honey – liquid	½ C	125 ml
Basil – dried	1 tsp	5 ml
Salt	1 tsp	5 ml
Pepper	½ tsp	2 ml
Water	½ C	125 ml
Garlic – minced	1 clove	
Brown sugar	1/4 C	60 ml

- Combine all ingredients in a saucepan and bring to a boil.
- Reduce heat and let simmer for approximately 30 minutes.
- Serves: 1 litre

Salad:

Spinach	5 C	1250 ml
(Romaine lettuce can be substituted)		
Almonds, toasted	¼ C	60 ml
Grapefruit slices, pink	½ C	125 ml
Red onion, chopped	¼ C	60 ml

- Toss together the above ingredients, and mix with the Raspberry vinaigrette.

- Serves: 5 – 7.

Romaine with Oranges and Pecans:

Salad:

Romaine Lettuce	2 heads	
(Wash and tear into bite size pieces)		
Mandarin orange pieces	½ C	125 ml
Pecan halves toasted	¾ - 1 C	175 ml
Red onion, chopped	¼ C	60 ml

Dressing:

Vinegar or Red wine vinegar	¼ C	50 ml
Granulated sugar	½ C	125 ml
Vegetable oil	½ C	125 ml
Salt	1 tsp	5 ml
Dijon mustard	1 tsp	5 ml
Water	2 tbsp	30 ml

- Place lettuce, oranges and pecans in a salad bowl.
- Combine remaining ingredients in a blender and blend well.
- Make ahead and refrigerate until ready to toss salad.

Sunshine Salad:

Orange flavoured gelatine	3 oz	85 g
Boiling water	1 C	250 ml
Concentrated orange juice	6 oz	170 g
Mandarin orange slices, drain well	10 oz	284 ml
(Reserve 4 – 5 for garnish)		
Lemon flavoured gelatine	3 oz	85 g
Boiling water	1 C	250 ml
Whipping cream	1 ¼ C	290 ml
Cream cheese, light and soft	4 oz	125 g

- Dissolve orange gelatine in a small bowl, using boiling water.

- Stir in concentrated orange juice and oranges (withhold 4 –5 orange slices for garnish).

- Pour in mould and chill.

- Occasionally stir to ensure mandarin orange slices remain floating in gelatine.

- Dissolve lemon gelatine in a small bowl, using boiling water. Chill this until it is the consistency of an egg white.

- Whip the cream until stiff. Withhold ¼ C for garnish and blend in the remaining whip cream with the cream cheese. Mix in lemon gelatine.

- Pour over the orange gelatine in the mould, and chill well.

- Un-mould on a plate (could use lettuce leaves to garnish plate). Use remaining whip cream and mandarin orange slices for garnish.

Soups

Broccoli Cheese Soup:

Onion, medium, chopped	½ C	125 ml
Butter or margarine	2 tbsp	30 ml
Milk	5 C	1250 ml
GF chicken bouillon powder	1 tsp	5 ml
Garlic cloves, minced	2	
Broccoli, fresh, chop to bite size	4 C	1000 ml
Salt	1 tsp	5 ml
Pepper	½ tsp	2 ml
Cheddar cheese, grated	1 C	250 ml

- In a large sauce pan, sauté onion and butter, until soft, add garlic and cook for 1 –2 minutes more. Careful not to burn the garlic or you will end up with a burnt taste to the soup.

- To the sauce pan add, milk, GF chicken bouillon, fresh broccoli, salt and pepper.

- Bring to a boil, stirring the mixture often to ensure it does not scorch.

- Reduce heat and cover until the broccoli is tender.

- Add cheese, stirring constantly until it is melted.

- Serves: 8 servings, approximately 1 C (250 ml) each

Butternut Squash Soup:

Garlic, head	1	
Onion, medium, chopped	1	
Olive oil	1 tbsp	15 ml
Potatoes, peeled and chopped	2	
Butternut squash	6 C	1500 g
GF Chicken broth	8 C	2000 g
Bay leaves	2	
Thyme,	1 tsp	5 ml
Salt	1 tsp	5 ml
Pepper	½ tsp	2 ml
Cream, half and half	½ C	125 ml

Preparing the squash, potatoes and garlic:

- Preheat oven to 375°F (190°C).

- Wash butternut squash, slice in quarters and pierce each section with fork, place on a lightly greased cookie sheet and bake for approximately 45 minutes or until tender.

- Remove the squash from the oven and using a large spoon scoop out the baked squash into a bowl and set aside.

- Prepare the head of garlic for baking by slicing off the top of the head of garlic and wrap in tin foil enough to wrap the head of garlic and bake for 45 minutes.

- Remove from the oven cut the top off and gently squeeze cloves out into a small bowl and set aside.

- Peel potatoes, dice and cook until tender, approximately 20 minutes, drain and set aside.

Preparing the soup:

- In a large sauce pan, heat the oil in the pan. Add onions and cook on a medium heat until they are soft, ensure that the pan is not too hot and burns the onions – cook for approximately 10 minutes.

- Combine the garlic, potatoes, squash, bay leaves and the stock and allow to cook on a slow boil for 25 minutes. Remove the bay leaves.

- Puree the soup in the blender and return it to the pot. Bring to a simmer then add the thyme, cream, salt and pepper.

- Serves: 8, approximately 1 C (250 ml) each

Notes:

➢ Topping with GF croutons that have been toasted in maple syrup. To make GF croutons, preheat oven to 350°F (180°C) degrees; then toast four pieces of GF bread, butter and slice into small bite size pieces, pour bite size pieces into a medium sized mixing bowl and drizzle with about 1/4 C of maple syrup, ensure well mixed; pour on to a lightly greased cookie sheet and bake for about 5 – 7 minutes.

Chicken Noodle Soup:

Water	6 C	1500 ml
Chicken parts, skin removed	4 pieces	
White wine, dry	1 C	250 ml
GF Chicken bouillon	2 cubes	
Onion, medium, chopped	1 C	250 ml
Celery, chopped	1 C	250 ml
Carrots, chopped	1 C	250 ml
Parsley flakes	¼ C	
Bay leaf	1	
Thyme	½ C	125 ml
Salt	1 tsp	5ml
Pepper	½ tsp	2 ml
Rice Noodles	½ pkg	

- In a large stockpot combine water, chicken parts and white wine and cook for 2 ½ hours.

- Remove any chicken bones from the soup base.

- Add to the chicken base the onion, celery, carrots, parsley flakes, bay leaf, thyme, salt, pepper and GF chicken bouillon cubes, and stir together.

- Bring to a boil and reduce heat to simmer, and cook for ½ hour.

- Using a kettle, bring to a boil enough water to cover the rice noodles in a large bowl, leave in bowl until soft.

- Add noodles to the chicken soup and stir together.

- Serves: 8.

Clam Chowder Soup:

Bacon, diced and cooked	½ pkg	
Ham, cooked and chopped	1 C	250 ml
Onion, medium, chopped	1 C	250 ml
Celery, chopped	1 C	250 ml
Potatoes, chopped	2 C	500 ml
Carrots, chopped	1 C	250 ml
Water	2 C	500 ml
Butter or margarine, melted	3/4 C	175 ml
GF flour mixture	1 C	250 ml
Salt	2 tsp	10 ml
Pepper	1 tsp	5 ml
Baby clams	10 oz	284 ml
Milk	8 C	2 litres
Cream (half and half)	1 C	250 ml

- Cook diced bacon, drain and set aside.

- Chop cooked ham, and set aside.

- In a large stockpot combine, onion, celery, carrots, potatoes, and water. Bring this mixture to a boil and reduce heat until vegetables are tender. May need to add more water to ensure vegetables do not burn.

- In a medium size pan, melt the butter or margarine, and add the GF flour mixture, slowly to ensure that mixture is not lumpy, stir until smooth.

- Add the salt and pepper to the GF flour mixture, and stir.

- Pour in slowly the GF flour mixture to the vegetables. More water (1 C or 250 ml) may be required to ensure mixture does not burn to the pot. Bring mixture a boil 1 – 2 minutes, and then reduce to a low heat for another 5 minutes, stirring constantly to prevent the mixture from burning.

- Add to the mixture the milk and cream. Stirring frequently to prevent the mixture setting on.

- Add in baby calms, ham and bacon and cook for another 10 minutes.

- Serves: 10.

Note:
➢ I usually freeze some (2 or 3 portions) of this recipe.

Minestrone Soup:

Bacon slices, cut in small pieces	4	
Onion, medium, chopped	½ C	125 ml
Ground beef, lean	1 ½ lbs	750 g
Boiling water	6 C	1.5 L
GF beef bouillon	2 cubes	
Canned spaghetti sauce	2 C	500 ml
Celery, chopped	1 C	250 ml
Carrots, medium, chopped	1 C	250 ml
Zucchini, chopped	1 C	250 ml
Oregano	¼ tsp	1ml
Salt	1 tsp	5 ml
Pepper	½ tsp	2 ml
Garlic powder	¼ tsp	1 ml
Kidney beans, with juice	14 oz	398 ml
GF pasta (corn elbow noodles)	1 C	250 ml

- In a large pot, sauté onion, bacon and ground beef, cook until bacon is cooked. Drain fat.

- Combine the water and GF beef bouillon cubes and dissolve by stirring. Add this to the ground beef mixture.

- Add in, spaghetti sauce, celery, carrots, zucchini, oregano, garlic powder, salt and pepper. Bring to a boil, reduce heat and let simmer for approximately 30 minutes.

- Add bean and pasta and bring to a boil for 10 more minutes

- Serves: 12 servings, approximately 1 C (250 ml) each.

Mushroom Soup:

Onion, medium, chopped	½ C	125 ml
Butter or margarine	¼ C	60 ml
Fresh mushrooms, chopped or sliced	2 C	500 ml
GF flour mixture	¼ C	60 ml
Salt	¼ tsp	1 ml
Pepper	¼ tsp	1 ml
Garlic cloves, minced	2	
GF beef bouillon	1 C	250 ml
GF chicken bouillon	1 C	250 ml
Boiling Water	2 C	500 ml
Milk	1 C	250 ml
Cream (half and half)	1 C	250 ml

- In a large pot, sauté onion, butter and mushrooms, until soft, add garlic and cook for a 1 –2 minutes more. Careful not to burn the garlic or you will end up with a burnt taste to the soup.

- Stir together the milk and GF flour mixture, ensure there are no lumps.

- To the mushroom add the GF flour milk mixture, salt and pepper; stirring constantly.

- In a two cup measuring cup dissolve beef and chicken stock, and add to pot.

- Over medium heat, bring to a boil, stirring often until mixture thickens.

- Add in cream and bring to a boil.

- Serves: 5, approximately 1 C (250 ml) each.

<u>Note:</u>

➤ I usually freeze some (2 or 3 portions) of this recipe and use this in making dishes calling for mushroom soup.

Wonton Soup:

Wonton:

Pork, ground	1/2 C	125 ml
Green onions, chopped	2 tbsp	30 ml
GF hoisin sauce	1 tbsp	15 ml
GF soya sauce	2 tsp	10 ml
Garlic cloves, minced	2	
Cornstarch	2 tsp	10 ml
Rice paper wrappers, small	16	

Soup:

Olive oil	2 tsp	10 ml
Carrots, diced	¼ C	60 ml
Green onions, chopped	¼ C	60 ml
Water	3 C	750 ml
Rice vinegar	2 tbsp	30 ml
Ginger, fresh minced peeled	2 tbsp	30 ml
Salt	¼ tsp	1 ml
Black pepper	¼ tsp	1 ml
GF chicken bouillon	48 oz	1500 g
Broccoli florets	1 C	250 ml
Snow Peas	1 C	250 ml

- Wonton preparation: mix together the ground pork, chopped green onions, GF hoisin sauce, GF soya sauce, minced garlic, and cornstarch.

- In a sauce pan ½ full of water heat until boiling and then reduce to simmer. This water will be used for dipping the rice paper wrappers for the won tons.

- Working with one wrapper at a time, dip the wrapper in the warm water, in a few seconds the wrapper will be come soft. Remove the wrapper with tongs from the water and place on working surface. Spoon on approximately 1 tsp of the mixture in the centre of the wrapper. Fold or twist wrapper around the pork mixture.

- Set wonton aside on a dish and cover with a damp cloth to prevent drying out of the wonton. Repeat process.

- Soup: Heat oil in a Dutch oven over medium high heat until hot.

- Add carrots and green onions and sauté until tender, approximately 3 minutes.

- Add water, vinegar, ginger, salt, pepper, and chicken broth, and bring to a boil.

- Add broccoli and snow peas and reduce heat to medium low.

- Add in wontons and let simmer for an additional 6 minutes.

- Serves: 8, approximately 1 ¼ C per serving.

Sweets – Desserts

Almond Cookies:

Butter or Margarine	1 C	250 ml
Granulated sugar	1 C	250 ml
Brown sugar	1 C	250 ml
Eggs	2	
Vanilla	½ tsp	2 ml
GF flour mixture	2 C	500 ml
Xanthan gum	2 tsp	10 ml
Salt	½ tsp	2 ml
Baking soda	1 tsp	5 ml
Slivered almonds	3 C	750 ml

- Preheat oven to 350°F (180°C).
- Grease cookie sheet, or cover with a piece of parchment paper.
- Cream together the butter or margarine, white and brown sugars.
- Beat in eggs
- Add in vanilla.
- Blend together the GF flour mixture, xanthan gum, salt, and baking soda.
- Mix GF flour mixture into the creamed butter and sugar mixture.
- Add shaved/slivered almonds.

- Using a teaspoon, drop spoonfuls of cookie mixture on to a lightly greased cookie sheet.

- Bake cookies for approximately 10 minutes, or until lightly brown.

- Yield: 6 dozen cookies.

Apple Crisp:

Filling:

Apples, peeled and sliced	5	
Granulated sugar	½ C	125 ml
GF flour mixture	1 tbsp	15 ml
Cinnamon	1 tbsp	15 ml

Topping:

Butter	¼ C	60 ml
GF flour mixture	1 C	250 ml
Brown sugar, packed	¼ C	60 ml
Salt	½ tsp	2 ml
Baking soda	¼ tsp	1 ml
GF baking powder	½ tsp	2 ml

- Preheat oven to 350°F (180 °C).

- Grease a 9 inch (23 cm) square baking dish

- Mix apples with sugar, GF flour mixture, and cinnamon, ensure well covered to prevent apples from browning. Pour into the baking dish.

- For the topping combine all topping ingredients, spread over apples and bake for 30 minutes.

- Serves: 7 – 9.

Note:

➢ This freezes very well, and can be made in advance.

Apple Pie with Crumble Topping:

Apples, Granny Smith, peeled and sliced	8	
Sugar	1/2 C	125 ml
Butter	2 tbsp	30 ml
Cinnamon, ground	½ tsp	3 ml
Cornstarch	1 tbsp	15 ml
Pie crust recipe, for one pie		

Topping Mixture:

Butter	¼ C	60 ml
GF flour mixture	1 C	250 ml
Brown sugar, packed	¼ C	60 ml
Salt	½ tsp	2 ml
Baking soda	¼ tsp	1 ml
GF baking powder	½ tsp	2 ml

- Preheat oven to 450 °F (230 °C).
- Make pie crust recipe. pg 42
- Peel, core and slice apples.
- In a large bowl combine the sugar, cinnamon and cornstarch, and add in apples covering completing to prevent them from turning brown.
- Prepare pie crust dough for an 8" (20 cm) baking dish.
- Place apple mixture in pie crust and dot butter a top the apple mixture.

- In a medium sized bowl combine the Topping Mixture ingredients, pour mixture overtop of apples, and place in oven.

- Bake for approximately 10 minutes and then reduce temperature to 350 °F (180 °C) for 50 – 60 minutes, until apples are tender and topping is light brown.

- Serves: 6 – 8.

Basic Vanilla Caramels

Sugar	2 C	500 ml
Butter	½ C	125 ml
Corn syrup	1 C	250 ml
Whipping cream	2 C	500 ml
Vanilla	1 tsp	5 ml

- Combine the sugar and corn syrup in heavy bottom pot and continuously stir on low heat (medium – to low). Boil this mixture until it reaches a softball stage.

- Add cream slowly as not to cool the mixture too quickly (so it never stops boiling), bring to a boil again and until the mixture reaches the softball stage again.

- Then add the butter in the same way the cream was added and bring the mixture to the softball stage.

- Remove from heat and add the vanilla.

- Mixture is ready for pouring into a 9 x 13 pan for soft caramels, or can be used as the medium for homemade turtles.

Brownies:

Butter or margarine	1 C	250 ml
Brown sugar, packed	2 C	500 ml
Eggs	4	
Vanilla	2 tsp	10 ml
GF flour mixture	1 C	250 ml
Xanthan gum	1 tsp	5 ml
Cocoa	½ C	125 ml
Walnuts or pecans, chopped, optional	1 C	250 ml

- Preheat oven to 300°F (150°C).
- Grease 9 x 13 x 1 ¾ (34 x 23 x 4 cm) baking pan.
- In a large bowl, cream together the butter or margarine, brown sugars.
- In a small bowl, lightly beat together the eggs then add in vanilla and add this mixture to creamed butter mixture.
- In a large bowl, blend together the GF flour mixture, cocoa and xanthan gum.
- Mix GF flour mixture into the creamed butter and sugar mixture.
- Blend in chopped walnuts if desired.
- Pour into pan, spread evenly.
- Bake 30 minutes or until passes the toothpick test.
- Serves: 10.

Carrot Cake and Cream Cheese Icing:

Granulated sugar	2 C	500 ml
GF flour mixture	2 C	500 ml
Xanthan gum	2 tsp	10 ml
GF Baking soda	2 tsp	10 ml
Cinnamon	2 tsp	10 ml
Salt	pinch	
Vegetable oil	1 ¼ C	300 ml
Shredded carrots	3 C	750 ml
Eggs, large	4 large	
Vanilla	2 tsp	10 ml
GF non-stick spray		

- Preheat oven to 350°F (180°C).
- Grease 9 x 13 x 1 ¾ inch (34 x 23 x 4 cm) cake pan.
- In a large bowl combine all the dry ingredients.
- Blend in the oil.
- Stir in the eggs, carrots and vanilla. Pour the batter into a cake pan.
- Bake for 45 – 50 minutes.
- Cool and ice with cream cheese icing list below
- Yield: 12 pieces.

Cream Cheese Icing

Cream cheese, softened	8 oz	250g
Butter or margarine, softened	½ C	125 ml
GF icing sugar	2 C	500 ml
Vanilla	1 tsp	5 ml

- In a medium sized mixing bowl whip the cream cheese, ensure there are no lumps.
- Blend in the softened butter or margarine, GF icing sugar and vanilla.
- Blend until smooth.
- Spread over the cooled carrot cake, and serve.

Chocolate Chip Cookies:

Butter or margarine, softened *(flaxseed, ground 1½ C)* *(olive oil ½ c)* — 1 C — 250 ml

GF flour mixture — 2 C — 500 ml

Xanthan gum — 2 tsp — 10 ml

Granulated sugar *(honey)* — 1 C — 250 ml

Brown sugar, packed *(molasses)* — ½ C — 125 ml

Baking soda — 2 tsp — 10 ml

Salt — 1 tsp — 5 ml

Egg, large, slightly beaten — 2

Vanilla — 2 tsp — 10 ml

milk ≈ ½ c → ¾ c

Chocolate chips — 2 C — 500 ml

hemp seeds ½ c

Quinoa flour 1¼ c

- Preheat oven to 350°F (180°C).

- Grease cookie sheets

- In a large bowl cream together granulated sugar, brown sugar, and butter or margarine. Then blend in egg and vanilla.

- In a medium bowl mix together the GF flour mixture, baking soda, xanthan gum and salt. Then slowly add this mixture to the creamed sugar and butter mixture.

- Mix in the chocolate chips.

- Using a teaspoon, drop dough on the cookie sheets, approximately 2 inches (5 cm) a part.

- Bake for approximately 10 – 12 minutes, or until a light golden brown in color.

- Serves: 48 cookies.

Cranberry, Raisin, Almond Cookies:

Butter or Margarine	1 C	250 ml
Granulated sugar	1 C	250 ml
Brown sugar	1 C	250 ml
Eggs	2	
Vanilla	½ tsp	2 ml
GF flour mixture	2 C	500 ml
Xanthan gum	2 tsp	10 ml
Salt	½ tsp	2 ml
Baking soda	1 tsp	5 ml
Slivered almonds	2 C	500 ml
Cranberries	1 C	250
Raisins	2 C	500 ml

- Preheat oven to 350°F (180°C).
- Grease cookie sheet, or cover with a piece of parchment paper.
- Rinse raisins in warm water, let soak until needed.
- Cream together the butter or margarine, white and brown sugars.
- Beat in eggs
- Add in vanilla.
- Blend together the GF flour mixture, xanthan gum, salt, and baking soda.

- Mix GF flour mixture into the creamed butter and sugar mixture.

- Add shaved/slivered almonds and cranberries and stir until well mixed.

- Drain raisins and add, stir until well mixed.

- Using a teaspoon, drop spoonfuls of cookie mixture on to a lightly greased cookie sheet.

- Bake cookies for approximately 10 minutes, or until lightly brown.

- Yield: 72 cookies.

Cream Puffs:

The Shells:

Water	1 C	250 ml
Butter	3 tbsp	45 ml
Granulated sugar	2 tsp	10 ml
Salt	¼ tsp	3 ml
GF flour mixture	1 C	250 ml
Xanthan gum	1 tsp	5 ml
Egg whites	3	
Eggs, large	3	

The Filling:

Whipping cream or packaged whipped topping	1 C	250 ml
GF icing sugar	2 tbsp	30 ml

Sprinkle with GF icing sugar before serving

- Preheat oven to 425°F (220°C).
- Cover a large, heavy baking sheet with parchment paper.
- In a large, heavy saucepan combine water, butter, granulated sugar, salt and bring to a boil over medium to high heat and stir occasionally with a wooden spoon.
- After bringing to a boil; remove from heat.

- Add in GF flour mixture and xanthan gum to water mixture, stirring well until smooth and mixture pulls away from sides of pan.

- Return pan to heat and cook for 30 seconds, stirring constantly.

- Remove pan from heat, and 3 eggs and egg whites, 1 at a time; using a hand mixer at medium speed until combined, for approximately 1 minute.

- Using a rubber spatula put the dough into 12 mounds (about 1/4 cup each) on the prepared cookie sheet; leave space between each mound to allow for rising.

- Bake at 425°F (220°C) for 20 minutes then reduce oven temperature to 350 degrees F (do not open oven door), and bake for another 20 minutes.

- Bake an additional 20 minutes. Turn oven off.

- Pierce the top of each puff with a knife and place the puffs back in the cooling oven for 20 minutes.

- Remove from oven; cool completely on a wire rack.

- Yield: 12

- For the filling, whip the whipping cream until stiff peaks are formed, and then and in the GF icing sugar; whip again for 30 seconds to ensure ingredients are well mixed.

- Slice open the cream puff body, and using a tablespoon, add approximately two spoonfuls to each cream puff.

- Sprinkle with GF icing sugar and serve.

- Yield: 12

Note:

➢ These cream puff bodies can be frozen for one month. Thaw before using.

Flat Bottom Fruit Pie:

Pie crust recipe, one pie

Sugar	1 tsp	5 ml
Cinnamon	¼ tsp	2 ml
Half and half cream	1 ½ C	375 ml
Whipped topping, (e.g. cool whip)	1 C	250 ml
Jell-O Vanilla Instant Pudding	1 pkg	
Peaches, sliced	1 ½ C	375 ml
Blueberries	½ C	125 ml
Raspberries	½ C	125 ml
Chocolate, semi sweet, grated	¼ C	60 ml

- Preheat oven to 400° F (200° C) degrees.

- Make pie crust recipe.

- Roll out pie crust recipe to a 9 x 9 inch (22 x 22 cm) circle and place on baking pan, cover with cinnamon and sugar.

- Place in oven and bake for 8 to 10 minutes, or until light brown. Remove from oven and cool completely.

- While pie crust is cooking, blend together in a large bowl the half and half cream and   Jell-O Vanilla pudding. Beat together for 2 minutes or until well blended, soft peaks form. Gently fold in the whipped topping, cover and refrigerate until ready to use.

- When ready to serve, cover pie crust with pudding mixture, and then top with fruit, cover with grated semi sweet chocolate.

- Serves: 8.

Fruit Topping:

Granulated sugar	1 C	250 ml
Water	1 C	250 ml
Fruit	1 ½ C	375 ml
(blueberries, raspberries, strawberries, etc.)		
Lemon juice	2 tbsp	30 ml
Cornstarch	2 tbsp	30 ml
Water	¼ C	60 ml

- In a medium sized saucepan, add in sugar, water, fruit, and lemon juice and bring to a boil, stirring constantly. Reduce heat.

- Mix together in a separate dish, cornstarch and cool water, and slowly stir into the saucepan mixture, stirring constantly.

- Bring mixture to a boil and cook until the mixture thickens; stirring constantly.

- Remove from burner and pour mixture into a heatproof bowl and cool/refrigerate until required.

Note:

➢ This sauce is quite versatile. It can be made ahead of time, covered, and refrigerated. You can serve it cold or at room temperature, or reheat it.

➢ The sauce can be served as a topping on ice cream or cheese cake.

Fudge Espresso Soufflé with Raspberry Sauce:

Unsweetened cocoa	1/2 cup	125 ml
Hot water	6 tbsp	90 ml
Instant espresso or 2 tablespoons or 30 ml of instant coffee granules	1 tbsp	15 ml
Butter or stick margarine	2 tbsp	30 ml
GF flour mixture	3 tbsp	45 ml
Milk – skim or 2%	3/4 C	175 ml
Granulated sugar	¼ C	60 ml
Salt	1/8 tsp	.5 ml
Egg whites	4 large	
Granulated sugar	3 tbsp	45 ml
GF non-stick spray		
Raspberry Sauce	1 recipe	

- Preheat oven to 375°F (190°C) degrees.
- Combine first 3 ingredients, stirring until smooth.
- Melt butter in a small, heavy saucepan over medium heat.
- Add GF flour mixture; cook 1 minute, stirring constantly with a whisk.
- Gradually add milk, granulated sugar, and salt; cook 3 minutes or until thick, stirring constantly.
- Remove from heat; stir in cocoa mixture.
- Spoon into a large bowl; cool slightly.

- Beat egg whites at high speed of a mixer until foamy. Add 3 tablespoons sugar, 1 tablespoon at a time, beating until stiff peaks form.

- Gently fold 1 cup egg white mixture into cocoa mixture; gently fold in remaining egg white mixture.

- Spoon into a 1-1/2-quart soufflé dish coated with GF non-stick spray.

- Bake at 375° for 45 minutes or until puffy and set.

- Make Raspberry Sauce recipe.

- Serve warm with Raspberry Sauce.

- Yield: 6 servings (serving size: 1 wedge and 2 tablespoons sauce).

Note:

➤ When this soufflé falls, the result is a dense fudge cake. Leftovers are great; they can be served at room temperature or chilled with the Raspberry Sauce.

Hawaiian Marshmallow Dessert:

Crust:

Butter or margarine, softened	½ C	125 ml
Coconut	¾ C	185 ml
Pecans or almonds chopped	¾ C	185 ml

Filling:

Marshmallows, miniature	3 ½ C	875 ml
Pineapple, crushed and drained	19 oz	540 gm
(reserve ½ C (125 ml) liquid		
Dream Whip	1 pkg	
Lemon juice	1 tbsp	15 ml

Topping:

Coconut	¼ C	60 ml
Pecan or almonds, chopped	¼ C	60 ml
Fresh fruit	½ C	125 ml

Crust:

- Preheat the oven to 350°F (180°C).

- In a medium sized bowl, melt the butter in a saucepan or microwave.

- Stir in coconut and nuts, and press into a 9 x 9 inch (22 cm) pan, and bake for 10 minutes or until crust is light brown, and cool.

<u>Filling</u>:

- In a large sauce pan melt marshmallows with lemon juice and the reserved pineapple liquid over low heat, stirring until smooth.

- Refrigerate until slight thickened, about 30 – 40 minutes.

- Prepare Dream Whip topping as per package instructions, and set aside in fridge until marshmallow mixture is cool.

- When marshmallow mixture is cooled, blend in the crushed pineapple and prepared dream Whip topping. Stir until well blended and pour over crust and set aside in refrigerator until firm, approximately 4 hours.

<u>Topping</u>:

- Mix together remaining coconut and pecans or almonds and sprinkle over top of cake.

- Garnish with sliced fruit, e.g. kiwi or oranges, etc.

- Serves: 9.

Homemade Turtles:

Nuts (pecans or cashews or almonds)	1 1b	500 g
Basic vanilla caramel recipe	1 recipe	
Chocolate, semi sweet	8 oz	250 g

- Lightly oil large baking sheet or cover baking sheet with parchment paper or wax paper.

- Pour nuts directly into caramel mixture and the scoop out of pot small mounds (about 4 nuts to a mound) and place on the greased cookie sheet or parchment paper.

- Let cool.

- While nuts and caramel mixture are cooling (10-15 minutes), melt chocolate in a double boiler and low heat. Patience is key to not burning the chocolate.

- After nut and caramel mixture has cooled spoon overtop of each mound the semi-sweet chocolate and allow time to cool.

- Yields: 60 turtles

Key Lime Pie:

Unflavoured gelatine powder	¼ oz	7 g
Cold Water	¼ C	50 ml
Egg yolks	4	
Granulated sugar	½ C	125 ml
Lime juice	1/3 c	75 ml
Salt	½ tsp	2 ml
Grated lime peel	2 tsp	10 ml
Green food coloring	3 dashes	
Egg whites	4	
Granulated sugar	½ C	125 ml
Whipping cream	2 C	500 ml
(Reserve 1 cup/250 ml for garnish)		
GF bake pie shell, (9 inch/22 cm)	1	

- Sprinkle gelatine over cold water in saucepan. Let stand 5 minutes.

- Add egg yolks and beat well. Add first amount of sugar, lime juice, salt, and lime peel. Beat to mix. Tint the mixture, using the green food coloring, to a light green. Heat and stir the mixture until boiling then remove from heat. Chill until mixture leaves a mound when spooned.

- Beat the egg whites until soft peaks form. Add second amounts of sugar gradually while continuing to beat until stiff peaks form. Fold gelatine mixture into egg whites.

- Whip cream until stiff, and then fold in 1 cup/250 ml into the mixture.

- Spoon mixture into baked pie shell and chill well.

- Garnish with remaining whip cream.

- Serves: 6 – 8.

Lemon Loaf:

Butter	1 ½ C	375 ml
Granulated sugar	3 C	750 ml
Eggs, large	6	
GF flour mixture	4 ½ C	1125 ml
GF baking powder	1 tbsp	15 ml
Grated lemon rind	4 tsp	20 ml
Milk (skim or 2%)	1 1/2 C	375 ml
Light sour cream	¾ C	175 ml
Xanthan gum	3 tsp	15 ml
Salt	3/4 tsp	7 ml

Lemon Glaze:

Lemon juice	½ C	125 ml
Granulated sugar	¾ C	175 ml

- Preheat oven to 350°F (180°C).
- Grease 3, 4 ½ x 8 ½ (10 x 20 cm) loaf pans.
- In a large bowl, cream together butter and sugar.
- Stir in eggs and lemon rind.
- Stir in light sour cream.
- In another bowl, combine GF flour mixture baking soda, salt and xanthan gum.
- To the sugar mixture, alternately add the dry ingredients and the milk until well blended. Be sure not to over mix.

- Pour batter into the 2 greased loaf pans.

- Bake for 45 – 55 minutes, or until successfully completes the toothpick test.

- Mix together lemon juice and sugar.

- Remove loaves from oven and top with lemon glaze.

- Return loves to oven and bake for an additional 5 minutes.

- Remove from oven, and let cool.

- Yield: 3 loaves

Light Cherry Cheesecake with a Nut Crust:

Crust:

Butter or margarine, softened	½ C	125 ml
Coconut	¾ C	185 ml
Pecans or almonds, finely chopped	¾ C	185 ml

Filling:

Light cream cheese, softened	8 oz	250 g
Granulated sugar	1 C	250 ml
1 package of whipped topping (e.g. Dream Whip)		
Lemon juice	1 tbsp	15 ml

Topping:

Cherry pie filling	19 oz	542 ml

Crust:

- Preheat the oven to 350°F (180°C).

- In a medium sized bowl, melt the butter in a saucepan or microwave.

- Stir in coconut and nuts, and press into a 9x 9 inch (22 cm) pan, and bake for 10 minutes or until crust is light brown, and cool.

<u>Filling</u>:

- In a large bowl, beat the cream cheese, sugar and lemon juice together to dissolve the sugar.

- In a separate bowl, make the whipped topping as per the directions on the package.

- Fold in the whipped topping into the cream cheese mixture, then spread over the crust and chill for a couple of hours and then spread the cherry pie filling mixture over the entire pan.

<u>Note:</u>

➢ If the topping is not suitable, or you have a particular fruit you would like to use, another option would be to make your own topping.

Lorraine's Upside Down Cake:

Batter:

Granulated sugar	1/2 C	125 ml
GF baking powder	1 tsp	5 ml
Milk (2%, 1% or skim)	1/4 C	60 ml
Butter, melted	¼ C	60 ml
Egg – lightly beaten	1 large	
GF flour mixture	7/8 C	235 ml

Upside down part:

Brown Sugar

Butter

Fruit, (your choice of sliced apples, or rhubarb, raspberries)

Cinnamon

- Preheat oven to 350°F (180°C).

- Grease a 9x9 inch (22 cm) baking dish,

- Into the greased baking dish sprinkle brown sugar, enough to cover the bottom of the pan, dot with butter and cover with a layer of fruit, and then sprinkle with cinnamon.

- For the batter, sift together GF flour mixture, GF baking powder, and sugar.

- Add in egg, melted butter, and milk.

- Beat until smooth and pour over fruit mixture.

- Bake for approximately 1 hour.

- Yield: 6 servings (serve upside down and with whipping cream or ice cream).

Christmas Reindeer Cookies *made Xmas 2010

Beat {
½ c butter
½ c peanut butter

Add vanilla mix {
¾ c honey
¼ tsp salt
¾ tsp baking soda
1 egg

½ tsp vanilla
1¼ c GF Flour -stir in
Choc chips,
red gum drops
Pretzels
crunchie sugar sprinkles

pretzels
choc chips
red gumdrop

Shape into balls, Flatten into triangles. Add decoration. Bake @ 375° for 7-9 min.

Molasses Ginger Cookies made Xmas 2010

½ c shortening
½ c honey
⅓ c molasses
2 eggs
1 ⅔ c GF. flour
1 tsp cinnamon
¼ tsp ginger
½ tsp baking soda.

& Flatten into 4" squares to make mini houses. Decorate w/ icing & candies. (on Christmas Eve.) Enjoy for breakfast on Christmas morning.)

187

Mix + Bake @ 375 for 10 min.

✶ Christmas Reindeer Cookies (see previous page)

Marshmallow Treats Squares: Rice Krispie Squares

Margarine or butter	¼ C	50 ml
Marshmallows (small)	5 C	1.25 L
or use (large)	40	
Vanilla (optional)	½ tsp	2 ml
GF rice crispies or GF corn flakes	7 C	1.75 L

- In a large saucepan melt margarine or butter over low heat. Add marshmallows stir until melted and well blended. Remove from heat.

- Stir in vanilla. Add GF Rice crispies, stirring until all are coated.

- Using a lightly greased spatula. Press into a greased 9 x13 x 1 ¾ inch (34 x 23 x 4 cm) pan. Cool and then cut into squares or other desired shapes.

- Yield: 12 squares.

Serve w/ custard sauce
or pg. 87, Christmas Creamy Pudding sauce
minute

Lemon Christmas Pudding (Carrot + Ginger)
✶ 1st made Xmas 2010

1 cup honey
1 cup beef suet
1 cup grated raw carrots
1 cup (2) " " potato
1 cup raisins
1 cup currants (or raisins, or nuts) slivered almonds
1 egg (2)
1 tsp salt
1 tsp baking soda
¼ cup lemon juice
½ cup flour (G.F.)
1 tsp xanthan gum

(1 Tbsp ginger (ground))?
4oz Candied ginger
(½ c)
¼ tsp nutmeg
¼ tsp cinnamon
188 ¼ tsp cloves
x ¼ cup milk

✶ Combine all ingredients. Mix well.

Steam in greased 2 qt casserole (use bundt pan) for 3 hrs.
Keep water ⅔ way up bundt pan (set on top of steaming ra
(to reheat, cover steam for 45 min

√ √G

Nellie's Christmas Cake (5 loaves) ← 1st made Xmas 2010

Butter, softened	1 lb	454 grams
~~Granulated sugar~~ Honey	2 C	500 ml
Eggs, large, beaten	12	
Grape jelly	1 ½ C	375 ml
GF flour mixture	5 C	1250 m
Xanthan gum	2 tbsp	30 ml
Baking soda	1 tsp	5 ml
GF baking powder	1 tsp	5 ml
Cinnamon	1 tbsp	15 ml
Nutmeg	1 tbsp	15 ml
Allspice	2 tsp	10 ml
Salt	½ tsp	2 ml
Mixed fruit, candied (dried apricots)	1 ½ lbs	900 g or candied zucchini, if have
Cherries, candied (dried (1lb) cranberries) + dried cherries (1/2)	1 ½ lbs	900 g
~~Vegetable oil~~ (applesauce)	1 ¼ C	300 ml
Pecans, roughly chopped (walnuts) sliPered almonds	1 lbs	500 g
Raisins	2 1lbs	900 g

- Preheat oven to 300°F (150°C). Turn on later.

- Wash raisins and set aside.

- Line 5 loaf pans with brown paper and then wax paper and grease and lightly with GF flour mixture.

- In a large bowl combine 2 cups of GF flour mixture with the candied cherries and mixed fruit, and set to the side.

189

- In a large bowl cream butter and add sugar beat again and then add the beaten eggs, mixing well.

- Add to the butter mixture half of the grape jelly and 1 cup of GF flour mixture and mix well.

- Add the remaining 2 cups of GF flour mixture, the baking soda, GF baking powder, cinnamon, nutmeg, all spice, salt and mix well. *+ Xanthan gum*

- To the candied fruit mixture add the raisins and chopped pecans, and mix well. *Add rest of grape jelly + applesauce N*

Turn → on oven Now 300°F

- Pour the butter mixture over the candied fruit mixture and mix well. *(wear gloves)*

- Pour the batter into the lined and greased loaf pans.

- Place in the oven with a pan of water, to prevent cakes from drying out.

- Bake for 3 hours or until done (maximum for 3 ½ hours). If cakes are cooked longer than 3 hours, cover with foil to prevent tops from over browning.

- Turn loaves out onto cooling racks and remove brown paper and wax paper.

- Yield: 5 loaves.

No Flour Chocolate Jelly Roll:

Cake base:

Egg whites, from large eggs	6	
Granulated sugar	¼ C	60 ml
Egg yolks, from large eggs	6	
Granulated sugar	½ C	125 ml
Cocoa powder	6 tbsp	90 ml
Vanilla	½ tsp	2 ml
GF icing sugar	¼ C	60 ml

Filling:

Semisweet chocolate	2/3 C	150 ml
Whipping cream	1 ½ C	325 ml
Vanilla	1 tsp	5 ml

Cake base:

- Preheat oven to 350°F (180°C).
- Grease and line a jelly roll pan or cookie sheet with sides, with wax paper or parchment paper.
- In large bowl, beat the egg whites until soft peaks form, and then slowly add the ¼ C   (60 ml) sugar until stiff.
- In a large bowl, beat together the egg yolks and ½ C (125 ml) of sugar until a lemon colour and light.
- Beat in the cocoa and vanilla.
- Fold in the egg white mixture.

191

- Spread in the prepared pan and bake for 15 to 20 minutes or until it passes the toothpick test.

- Lay out a clean tea towel and sift the GF icing sugar all over the towel. Turn cake out on top of the towel and remove the paper.

- Starting at one end of the towel, roll the cake and towel together to cool. When cool, unroll and spread on filling. Ensure the cake is completely cool before adding filling otherwise filling will begin to melt.

Filling:

- Melt the chocolate in a small saucepan over a double boiler on low heat or in a microwave. Do not let chocolate get to hot as the chocolate may burn.

- Spread the chocolate evenly over the cake.

- In a medium size bowl, add whip cream and vanilla, whip together until stiff peaks form, (saving some for garnishing) and then spread evenly over the cake.

- Roll cake again, and garnish with some seasonal berries and remainder of whip cream.

Note:

➢ If rolling of the cake does not work another option would be to carefully cut the cake into equal segments (thirds), and on a serving dish, place a segment of the cake on the bottom and cover with whipping cream, repeating the process until there are three layers of cake and whip cream.

Pavlova:

Egg whites, large	4	
Granulated sugar	1 C	250 ml
Cornstarch	1 tsp	4 ml
Vinegar	1 tsp	4 ml
Vanilla	1 tsp	4 ml

- Preheat oven to 350°F (180°C).
- Line a cookie sheet with a piece of foil in a nine inch circle.
- Beat egg whites until soft peaks form.
- Add sugar and cornstarch gradually beating until stiff. Texture should be smooth not grainy.
- Spread meringue in circle.
- Bake for 50 – 60 minutes. Turn oven off and let stand in oven for approximately 1 more hour.
- Peel off foil and cover with topping.

Topping:

Whipping cream	1 C	250 ml
Granulated sugar	2 tbsp	30 ml
Vanilla	1 tsp	5 ml
Fruit – sliced	2 C	500 ml
(Of your choice)		
Fruit glaze	1 recipe (below)	

- Whip cream until stiff, and then add sugar and vanilla.

- Spread over meringue.

- Arrange fruit on top of whipping cream mixture.

- Pour fruit glaze over top of fruit.

- Serves: 7 – 10.

<u>Simple Fruit Glaze:</u>

Granulated sugar	¼ C	60 ml
Water		
Cornstarch	1 ½ tsp	7 ml

- In a small saucepan, add sugar, water and cornstarch, stir constantly, bring to a boil until thick, remove from burner and cool.

- Paint fruit to seal and shine.

Pecan Brittle:

Corn Syrup	1 C	250 ml
Granulated sugar	2 C	500 ml
Water	½ C	125 ml
Margarine or Butter	¼ C	60 ml
Pecans, toasted and coarsely chopped	2 C	500 ml
Vanilla	1 tsp	5 ml
Baking Soda	2 tsp	10 ml

- Grease large cookie sheet with sides and set aside.
- In a large, heavy saucepan add, corn syrup, Granulated sugar and water. Bring to a boil and ensure sugar is dissolved. Stirring often, boil mixture until it reaches a softball stage or 235 F (112 C).
- To the mixture add, margarine or butter and pecans, and continue boiling until a hard crack stage is reached or 300 F (150 C). Stir constantly to prevent scorching.
- Once hard crack stage is reached, stir in vanilla and baking soda. This mixture will begin to foam; while foaming pour mixture out on to greased cookie sheet.
- Cool
- To serve break in to small sections.
- Yield: approximately 2 lbs (1000 g)

Puffed Rice Squares:

Margarine or Butter	1 C	250 ml
Corn Syrup	1 C	250 ml
Granulated sugar	1 C	250 ml
Cocoa	3 tbsp	45 ml
GF Puffed Rice	10 C	2.5 L

- In a large saucepan melt margarine or butter, corn syrup, sugar and cocoa. Over medium heat, bring to a soft ball and remove from heat. Do not leave unattended as mixture may burn to bottom of pan.

- Stir in GF puffed rice, stirring until all are coated.

- Using a lightly greased spatula. Press into a greased 9 x13 x 1 ¾ inch (34 x 23 x 4 cm) pan. Cool and then cut into squares or other desired shapes.

- Yield: 12 squares.

Rolled Rice Raisin Cookies:

Butter or margarine, softened	3/4 C	175 ml
GF flour mixture	1 ¼ C	310 ml
Xanthan gum	1 tbsp	15 ml
Granulated sugar	½ C	125 ml
Brown sugar, packed	1 C	250 ml
Baking soda	1 tsp	5 ml
Salt	½ tsp	2 ml
Cinnamon	1 tsp	5 ml
Egg, large, slightly beaten	1	
Water	2 tbsp	30 ml
Vanilla	2 tsp	10 ml
Brown rice flakes	3 C	750 ml
Raisins	1 ½ C	325 ml

- Preheat oven to 350°F (180°C).

- Grease cookie sheets.

- Wash raisins.

- In a large bowl cream together granulated sugar, brown sugar, and butter or margarine. Then blend in egg, water and vanilla.

- Add in GF flour mixture, baking soda, cinnamon, xanthan gum and salt, and mix together well.

- Mix in the raisins and brown rice flakes.

- Using a teaspoon, drop dough on the cookie sheets, approximately 2 inches (5 cm) a part.

- Bake for approximately 10 – 12 minutes.

- Serves: 48 cookies.

Rhubarb Coffee Cake:

Butter	½ C	125 ml
Brown Sugar, packed	1 ½ C	375 ml
Eggs, large	2	
GF flour mixture	2 C	500 ml
GF baking soda	1 ½ tsp	7 ml
Rhubarb – diced	3 C	750 ml
Milk (skim or 2%) sour	1 C	250 ml
Xanthan gum	2 tsp	10 ml

Topping:

Granulated sugar	½ C	125 ml
Cinnamon	2 tsp	10 ml

- Preheat oven to 350°F (180°C).
- Grease 9 x 13 x 1 ¾ inch (34 x 23 x 4 cm) baking dish.
- In a large bowl, cream together butter, brown sugar and egg.
- In another bowl, combine GF flour mixture baking soda, salt and xanthan gum.
- Mix in rhubarb into GF flour mixture, and then add butter mixture and the sour milk.
- Pour batter into greased baking dish.
- Mix together sugar and cinnamon and sprinkle over top of batter.

199

- Bake for 35 – 45 minutes, or until successfully completes the toothpick test.

- Yield: 12 servings

Note:

➤ To sour milk add 1 tsp (15 ml) of vinegar or lemon juice into a 1 C (250 ml) measuring cup and fill the remainder of the measuring cup with milk.

Rhubarb Pie with Crumble Topping:

Rhubarb, chopped	3 C	750 ml
Sugar	1 C	2502 ml
Cornstarch	3 tbsp	45 ml
Egg	1	

Pie crust recipe, for one pie

Topping Mixture:

Butter	¼ C	60 ml
GF flour mixture	1 C	250 ml
Brown sugar, packed	¼ C	60 ml
Salt	½ tsp	2 ml
Baking soda	¼ tsp	1 ml
GF baking powder	½ tsp	2 ml

- Preheat oven to 450°F (230°C).
- Clean and chop rhubarb.
- In a large bowl combine the sugar, cornstarch, and egg, then add in rhubarb and toss to ensure well coated in sugar mixture.
- Prepare pie crust dough for an 8" (20 cm) baking dish.
- Place rhubarb mixture in pie crust.
- In a medium sized bowl combine the Topping Mixture ingredients, pour mixture overtop of apples, and place in oven.

- Bake for approximately 10 minutes and then reduce temperature to 350°F (180°C) for the 45 – 50 minutes, until rhubarb is cooked and topping is light brown.

- Serves: 6 – 8.

Vegetables

Asparagus with Almonds:

Almonds – slivered	½ C	125 ml
Margarine or Butter	1 tbsp	15 ml
Asparagus, diagonally sliced	4 C	1 litre
Onion, chopped	½ C	125 ml
Pepper	to taste	
White wine, dry	2 tbsp	25 ml

(or chicken stock/broth)

- Rinse and trim asparagus.
- In a non-stick skillet, cook almonds, in margarine or butter until lightly browned; remove almonds and set aside.
- Add asparagus and onion and sauté; season with pepper and cook 3 – 5 minutes. .
- Add wine and cook covered for 2 minutes. .
- Transfer to serving dish and sprinkle with almonds. .
- Serves: 4 – 6.

Asparagus with Parmesan Basil Butter:

Butter, room temperature	¼ C	60 ml
Asparagus	1 lb	500 g
Parmesan cheese, grated	½ C	125 ml
Basil, dried	1 tsp	5 ml
Lemon juice	1 ½ tsp	7 ml
Garlic, finely chopped	1	
Pepper, freshly ground	to taste	
Salt	¼ tsp	1 ml
Water	1 C	250 ml

- Preheat the broiler of the oven.

- Rinse and snap off the stalks of the asparagus.

- In a non-stick skillet, bring to a boil 1 C of water with ¼ tsp of salt. Add asparagus spears to the water and cook for 3 – 4 minutes, until the asparagus is tender-crisp.

- Remove the asparagus from the water and run through a cold water bath to stop the cooking process.

- In an oven proof platter place the asparagus.

- In a medium sized bowl beat the butter until fluffy (can use a hand mixer or food process, or by hand depending preference).

- Add to the butter the Parmesan cheese, basil, lemon juice and ground pepper, and garlic, beat until well mixed.

- Spoon the butter mixture over the asparagus.

- Put the asparagus under the broiler for approximately 2 – 3 minutes or until the topping is light brown. Be careful not to over cook.

- Serve immediately.

- Serves: 4.

Baked Asparagus:

Asparagus	1 - 1½ lbs	500 – 750
Butter/Margarine	3 tbsp	45 ml
Lemon juice	2 tbsp	30 ml
Salt	to taste	
Pepper	to taste	

- Preheat oven to 350°F (180°C).
- Rinse and trim asparagus, do not peel.
- Arrange asparagus in a shallow dish in one or two layers.
- Dot with butter/margarine and lemon juice.
- Cover tightly with foil and bake for approximately 15 minutes.
- Serves: 4.

Baked Cauliflower:

Cheddar cheese, shredded	½ C	125 ml
Milk	1 C	250 ml
Cornstarch	2 tbsp	30 ml
Salt	1/2 tsp	2 ml
Pepper	to taste	
GF non-stick spray		
Cauliflower	4 C	1000 ml
GF bread crumbs	½ C	125 ml
Parmesan cheese	½ C	125 ml

- Preheat oven to 350°F (180°C).

- In a microwavable medium sized bowl or 2 C (500 ml) measuring cup, combine milk, cornstarch, salt and pepper and stir together.

- Place in microwave, on high, for 2 minutes, remove and stir, return to microwave for 1 - 2 more minutes. As the mixture blends it will become thick. Add cheddar cheese, stir, and return to microwave for 1 – 2 minutes, until the cheese has melted. Remove and set aside.

- Spray an oven proof dish with GF non-stick spray, pour in cauliflower into the dish and over with cheese sauce.

- Cover the cheese sauce with bread crumbs and Parmesan cheese. Place in oven and for 1 hour.

- Remove from oven and serve._

- Serves: 4._

Broccoli with Almond-Bread Crumb Topping:

Broccoli	6 C	1500 ml
GF Bread crumb	1/3 C	75 ml
Parmesan cheese	2 tbsp	30 ml
Almonds, finely chopped	2 tbsp	30 ml
Basil, dried	1 tsp	5 ml
Oregano, dried	1 tsp	5 ml
Salt	¼ tsp	1 ml
Black pepper	¼ tsp	1 ml

- Preheat oven to 450°F (230°C).
- Cook the broccoli in water for 2 minutes and drain. Rinse with cold water.
- Place broccoli in a casserole dish 11 x 7 inch, cm.
- Combine breadcrumbs and remaining ingredients and sprinkle bread crumb mixture evenly over broccoli.
- Bake for 15 minutes or until breadcrumb mixture is golden brown.
- Yield: 8 servings.

Broccoli Cakes:

Broccoli, fresh	4 C	1000 ml
Green onions	½ C	125 ml
Butter	3 tbsp	45 ml
Eggs, large	2	
Milk – skim or 2%	1 ½ C	375 ml
GF bread crumbs	¾ C	175 ml
Parmesan cheese	½ C	125 ml
Salt	½ tsp	2 ml
Pepper	½ tsp	2 ml
Nutmeg	¼ tsp	1 ml

- Preheat oven to 350°F (180°C).
- Grease 16 large muffin tins.
- Cook broccoli and drain well.
- Sauté onions in butter until soft; combine with remaining ingredients. Fill muffin tins and bake 20 – 25 minutes or until tested with a toothpick and toothpick comes out clean.
- Remove from muffin tins, and place on serving plate and serve.

Note:

➢ Other vegetables that taste great in this are: mushrooms, red pepper. This dish is good heated up again the next day.

Broccoli, Cauliflower, Carrots with Toasted Almonds:

Almonds, sliced	¼ C	60 ml
Carrots, diagonally cut	2 C	500 ml
Broccoli, florets	3 C	750 ml
Cauliflower, florets	2 C	500 ml
Butter	1 tbsp	15 ml
Green onions, finely chopped	¼ C	60 ml
Chicken stock	½ C	125 ml
Salt	½ tsp	2 ml
Black pepper, ground	1/4 tsp	1 ml

- Preheat oven to 350°F (180°C).

- Spread almonds in a single layer in a shallow pan. Bake at 350°F (180°C) for 7 minutes or until lightly browned and fragrant, stirring occasionally. Cool completely, and set aside.

- Place carrots in a large saucepan of boiling water; cook 3 minutes. Remove with a slotted spoon. Plunge into ice water, and drain.

- Place broccoli in boiling water; cook 2 minutes. Drain and plunge into ice water and drain.

- Place cauliflower in boiling water; cook 2 minutes. Drain and plunge into ice water and drain.

- Melt the butter in a 12-inch non-stick skillet over medium-high heat. Add the green onions and sauté for 2 minutes or until tender.

212

- Reduce heat to medium. Add carrots, broccoli, cauliflower and chicken stock, salt, and pepper; cover and cook 6 minutes or until carrots, broccoli and cauliflower are crisp-tender.

- Sprinkle with almonds. Serve immediately.

- Serves: 8.

Cauliflower Vinaigrette:

Cauliflower, medium head,	1	
Butter/Margarine	3 tbsp	45 ml
Lemon juice or vinegar	3 tbsp	45 ml

- Rinse and cut cauliflower into pieces.
- Cook cauliflower (boil or steam), and drain.
- Melt butter/margarine, and add lemon juice or vinegar, stir together.
- Pour over freshly cooked cauliflower and serve.
- Serves: 5.

Donna's Broccoli and Carrots with Dijon Sauce:

Broccoli	2 1bs	1 kg
Carrots	1 1b	500 g
Onion, chopped	¼ C	60 ml
Mozzarella Cheese	1 C	250 ml
Parmesan cheese	1/3 C	75 ml
Salt	pinch	

- Rinse and slice broccoli; peel broccoli stalks and cut into uniform diagonal slices. Separate heads into florets.
- Steam until tender/crisp. Drain and immerse in cold water.
- Rinse and peel carrot; cut into uniform diagonal slices.
- Cook in salted water until tender. Drain and cool.
- Set aside and make Dijon sauce.

Dijon Sauce:

Olive oil	½ C	125 ml
Mayonnaise	¼ C	60 ml
Red wine vinegar	2 tbsp	30 ml
Lemon juice	2 tbsp	30 ml
Dijon mustard	2 tbsp	30 ml
Garlic, minced	1 clove	
Salt and Pepper	to taste	

- Whisk together the sauce ingredients into a bowl.

- To serve: mix together broccoli, carrots, chopped onion and cheese.

- Pour sauce over the broccoli carrot mixture and mix together.

- Serves: 6.

Fanned Baked Potatoes:

Potatoes, large	4	
Salt	½ tsp	2 ml
Butter, melted	3 tbsp	45 ml
Parsley, chopped	1 tbsp	15 ml
Chives, chopped	1 – 2 tbsp	15 – 30 ml
Cheddar cheese, shredded	½ C	125 ml
Parmesan cheese	¼ C	60 ml

- Preheat oven to 425°F (220°C).

- Peel potatoes. Cut potatoes into thin slices; be careful not to cut through the potato. A long wooden skewer can be inserted into the potatoes to use as a guide to prevent cutting through the potato, removing after you have cut the potato, or the handle of a wooden spoon can also be used as a guide to prevent the cutting through.

- Place potatoes in a baking dish, and slightly fan potatoes.

- Drizzle the butter over the potatoes and sprinkle with salt.

- Sprinkle on the chopped parsley and chives.

- Bake the potatoes for approximately 40 – 50 minutes.

- Remove from oven and cover with the cheddar and Parmesan cheeses.

- Return to oven until the cheeses are light brown, approximately 10 minutes.

- Remove from oven and serve.

- Serves: 4.

Garlic Mashed Potatoes:

Potatoes – peeled and cubed	7 C	1750 g
Garlic, whole	6 cloves	
Milk – skim milk/2%	½ C	125 ml
Parmesan cheese	¼ C	60 ml
Butter or Margarine	2 tbsp	30 ml
Salt	½ tsp	2 ml
Pepper	to taste	

- Place potatoes and garlic in a saucepan. Cover with water; bring to a boil. Reduce heat. Simmer 20 minutes; or until tender with a fork; drain.

- In saucepan, add remaining ingredients and beat at medium speed of a mixer until smooth.

- Serves: 8, (3/4 C each or 175 ml).

Glazed Cucumbers:

Butter or margarine	¼ C	60 ml
Granulated sugar	3 tbsp	45 ml
Cucumbers, medium	2	
Salt	pinch	

- Peel cucumbers and slice diagonally, approximately ¼ inch slices

- Remove seeds from center of cucumber using the end of a teaspoon. Melt butter or margarine in a large non-stick skillet over medium heat; add sugar stirring until melted.

- Add cucumbers and salt and sauté for 4 – 5 minutes.

- Place into a serving bowl and serve.

- Serves: 6

Glazed Julienne Carrots:

Butter or Margarine	2 tbsp	30 ml
Brown sugar, packed	¼ C	60 ml
Carrots, julienne cut,	4 C	1000 ml
Salt	¼ tsp	2 ml
Pepper	¼ tsp	2 ml
Parsley, dried	2 tsp	10 ml

- Melt butter or margarine in a large non-stick skillet over medium heat; add brown sugar stir until melted._

- Add carrots, salt and pepper and cook 10 minutes or until carrots are crisp-tender, stir occasionally.

- Remove from heat; stir in parsley and serve._

- Serves: 8

Green Bean Casserole:

GF Mushroom soup	8 oz	235 ml
Milk	½ C	125 ml
GF soya sauce	1 tsp	5 ml
Green beans, drained	29 oz	426 ml
Pepper	to taste	
Onion, chopped	½ C	125 ml
Bread crumbs	½ C	125 ml
Parmesan cheese	½ C	125 ml

- Preheat oven to 350°F (180°C).

- In a 2 quart casserole dish, combine GF mushroom soup, milk, GF soya sauce and pepper, stir until smooth.

- Mix in green beans and onions.

- Cover the green bean mixture with bread crumbs and Parmesan cheese. Place in oven and for bake for 25 minutes.

- Remove from oven and serve.

- Serves: 6-8.

Green Beans with Almonds:

Almonds – slivered	¼ C	50 ml
Butter or margarine	2 tbsp	30 ml
Green beans	1 lb	500 g
Green onion, chopped	3	
Red pimento, chopped (optional)	2 tsp	8 ml
Salt	to taste	
Pepper	to taste	

- Rinse and trim ends off of green beans. Cook until tender, and then cool.

- Put butter and almonds into a frying pan, cook until golden brown. Ensure constantly stirring to avoid burning of almonds.

- Add onions and beans, salt and pepper and add pimento for color.

- Cook for approximately 5 more minutes and serve.

- Serves: 4 – 6.

Grilled Vegetables with Balsamic Vinaigrette:

Balsamic vinegar	1/4 cup	60 ml
Honey	2 tbsp	30 ml
Olive oil	1 tbsp	15 ml
Black pepper, coarsely ground	1 tsp	5 ml
Salt	½ tsp	2 ml
Garlic, minced	4 cloves	
Tomatoes, plum type and halved	4	
Zucchini, cut lengthwise into ¼ inch slices	2	
Red bell pepper, cut into 8 wedges	1	
Onion, cut into 2-inch-thick wedges	1	
GF non-stick spray		

- Combine first 6 ingredients in a bowl.
- Combine ingredients, tomatoes through onion, in a bowl.
- Divide balsamic vinaigrette and vegetable mixture evenly between 2 large zip-top plastic bags and seal.
- Marinate in refrigerator 1 hour, turning bags occasionally.
- Remove vegetables from bags; reserve marinade.
- Prepare grill.
- Place vegetables on grill rack coated with GF non-stick spray; grill 7 minutes on each side or until onion is tender, basting with reserved marinade.
- Yield: 8 servings (serving size: 1 cup or 250 ml).

Mashed Potatoes:

Potatoes, peeled and cubed	3 lbs	1.36 kg
Butter	3 tbsp	45 ml
Sour cream, low fat	½ C	125 ml
Salt	1 tsp	5 ml
Black pepper	½ tsp	2 ml
Milk, skimmed	¼ C	60 ml

- Put potatoes in a saucepan, and cover with water.
- Bring to a boil and reduce heat; simmer for approximately 15 minutes or until tender when pierced with a fork.
- Drain thoroughly.
- Add sour cream, butter and the milk, and mash to desired consistency.
- Add salt and pepper, and serve.
- Yield: 8.

Notes:

➢ Save the potato water and use in place of water when making gravy. Adds a nice flavour to the gravy.

➢ Potatoes can be mashed a variety of ways: a hand masher, by using a hand mixer, or by using a potato ricer – my preference is to use the potato ricer as it makes the potatoes a nice smooth texture.

Pam's Sautéed Zucchini:

Zucchini, medium, sliced	2	
Butter/Margarine	3 tbsp	45 ml
Small onion, thinly sliced	1	
Garlic, minced,	2 cloves	
Parmesan cheese	1/3 C	75 ml
Salt and pepper	to taste	

- Rinse and slice zucchini in to thin rounds.

- Peel and slice onion into thin rounds.

- Melt butter/margarine in non-stick frying pan.

- Sauté onion until opaque, and then add garlic, sauté for a minute or two more.

- Add in zucchini and cook until slightly tender.

- Reduce heat and cover with salt and pepper and with Parmesan cheese, then cover with a lid until cheese melts, stir occasionally (approximately 5 minutes), depending on taste you may want to add an additional tablespoon of butter at this point.

- Once cheese has melted, remove from stove and serve warm.

- Serves: 4.

Potato Dressing:

A nice change to the traditional bread dressings, serve with chicken or turkey.

Potatoes, large, cubed	6	
Margarine or butter	¼ C	60 ml
Bread GF	2 slices	
Onion, large, chopped	1 large	
Granulated sugar	1 tbsp	15 ml
Brown sugar, packed	1 tbsp	15 ml
Savory	1 tbsp	15 ml
Fancy molasses	1 tbsp	15 ml
White vinegar	1 tsp	5 ml
Salt	1/2 tsp	2 ml
Pepper	1/4 tsp	1 ml

- Peel and cook potatoes, when cooked thoroughly mash potatoes.
- Sauté onions in margarine and add granulated and brown sugars and add to mashed potatoes.
- Add remaining ingredients, and blend well.
- Pour potatoe mixture into a loaf pan and refrigerate until needed.
- To serve slice and serve
- Serves: 6 – 8

Roasted Broccoli with Garlic:

Olive oil	1 tbsp	15 ml
Broccoli, florets	6 C	1500 ml
Lemon peel	1 tsp	5 ml
Garlic cloves, chopped	2	
Salt	1/4 tsp	1 ml
Black pepper, ground	1/4 tsp	1 ml

- Preheat oven to 425°F (220°C).

- Grease a rimmed baking sheet.

- Combine in large bowl olive oil, lemon peel, salt, pepper, and garlic.

- Add to the above mixture the broccoli and toss until covered.

- Place broccoli in a single layer on the prepared rimmed baking sheet.

- Bake for 15 minutes or until tender, uncovered.

- Serves: 4 - 6.

Roasted Parsnips with Maple Syrup:

Olive oil	1 tbsp	15 ml
Parsnips, peeled	3	
Maple syrup	1 tbsp	15 ml
Salt	1/2 tsp	2 ml
Pepper, freshly ground	¼ tsp	1 ml

- Preheat oven to 450°F (230°C).
- Grease a rimmed baking sheet.
- Slice each parsnip into finger sized pieces, approximately 5 cups (1250 ml).
- Using a large bowl combine oil, salt and pepper, then add in the parsnip pieces and cover.
- Place parsnips in a single layer on the prepared rimmed baking sheet.
- Bake uncovered for 25 – 30 minutes or until tender and light brown.
- Remove from oven and drizzle with maple syrup to coat.
- Serves: 4 - 6.

Scalloped Potatoes:

Potatoes, medium peeled, sliced	6 – 8	
Onion, finely chopped	¼ C	60 ml
GF flour mixture	1/3 C	75 ml
Salt	1 ½ tsp	7 ml
Pepper	¼ tsp	1 ml
Milk	2 C	500 ml

Options:

Cheddar cheese, shredded	½ C	125 ml
Garlic, minced	2 cloves	
Parmesan cheese	¼ C	60 ml

- Preheat oven to 350°F (180°C).

- Grease a 2 quart/ casserole dish.

- Place half of the sliced potatoes in the bottom of the dish. Sprinkle with half of the chopped onion. If adding any of the options, add in half of the ingredient(s).

- Stir together milk, salt, pepper and GF flour mixture.

- Pour half of the milk mixture over the potatoes and onion.

- Repeat the next layer of the potatoes and onions, along with any of the options. Prior to adding the remaining milk mixture stir prior to pouring over the potato and onion mixture.

- Cover and bake for approximately 1 hour. Uncover and cook for another 30 minutes or until potatoes are done.

- Serves: 6.

Sweet and White Potato Spears:

Baking potatoes, cut into spears	3	
Sweet potatoes, cut into spears	3	
Italian dressing	½ C	125 ml
Parmesan cheese, grated	¼ C	60 ml
Parsley	2 tbsp	30 ml

- Preheat oven to 350°F (180°C).

- Lightly grease a rimmed baking sheet.

- Toss the potato spears in the Italian dressing, and place on baking sheet.

- Place in oven, and cook for 30 minutes, turn, and then cook for another 30 minutes.

- In the last 5 minutes cover with the parmesan cheese.

- Remove from oven and sprinkle the parsley over the potatoes prior to serving.

- Serves: 6 - 8.

Index

Page